WITHDRAWN
UTSA Libraries

Eyewitness Accounts of the American Revolution

The Revolutionary Journal of Col. Jeduthan Baldwin 1775-1778

The New York Times & Arno Press

Reprint Edition 1971 by Arno Press Inc.

*

LC# 73-140853
ISBN 0-405-01223-3

*

Eyewitness Accounts of the American Revolution, Series III
ISBN for complete set: 0-405-01187-3

*

Manufactured in the United States of America

THE REVOLUTIONARY JOURNAL OF
COL. JEDUTHAN BALDWIN
1775-1778

THE BALDWIN HOUSE, NORTH WOBURN, MASS.
Built in 1640 by Henry Baldwin, Grandfather of Col. Jeduthan Baldwin

THE

REVOLUTIONARY JOURNAL

OF COL. JEDUTHAN BALDWIN
1775-1778

EDITED WITH A MEMOIR AND NOTES BY
THOMAS WILLIAMS BALDWIN

SEAL OF RICHARD DE BURY

BANGOR
PRINTED FOR THE DE BURIANS
1906

Copyright 1906
BY THE DE BURIANS, BANGOR, MAINE
All Rights Reserved

The military reservation at Sabino Head, mouth of the Kennebec River, Maine, is to be named Fort Baldwin, in honor of Colonel Jeduthan Baldwin, Engineers and Artillery Artificer Regiment, Continental Army, who died June 4, 1788. — *By order of the Secretary of War, J. C. Bates, Major General, Chief of Staff, Washington, January 25, 1906.*

EDITION OF TWO HUNDRED COPIES.
THIS COPY IS NUMBER

THIS VOLUME IS DEDICATED
TO THE MEMORY OF

Col. Jeduthan Baldwin

"A TRUE PATRIOT AND AN INTREPID SOLDIER WHO
DID VALIANT SERVICE IN THE WAR OF
THE REVOLUTION"

INTRODUCTION

EVER since the existence of the MS. of the Journal contained in this volume became known to members of The De Burians, it has been their great desire to print the same as one of their publications. After many delays the Committee of Publication has great pleasure in issuing the same as the Third Volume in their series of works inscribed to the memory of Richard De Bury, Bishop of Durham, 1287–1345.

On December 8, 1897, a loan exhibition of rare articles of vertu, historic relics, art pieces, old lace, etc., was held at the residence of the Misses Baldwin in this city for the benefit of the Woman's Exchange. The original MS. of this Revolution Journal of Col. Baldwin, was one of the choice things exhibited at that time.

This MS. is now in possession of Miss Charlotte A. Baldwin, State Regent of the Maine Council of Daughters of the American Revolution. It formerly belonged to Thomas Williams Baldwin, Miss Baldwin's father, who inherited it from her grandfather, Luke Baldwin, a son of Col. Jeduthan Baldwin. Miss Baldwin does not remember when her father did not have this MS. and recalls many times when he took it from his desk and read some portions of it.

The Journal as now printed receives new interest from the fact that by order of the War Department of January 25, 1906, the Military Reservation at Sabino Head, at the mouth of the Kennebec River, in Maine, is named Fort Baldwin, in honor of this notable Military Engineer of the Revolution. The fort to be constructed at Sabino Head is to be located back of Fort Popham on the site of Popham's Fort St. George of 1607. The site was determined by a plan found in the general archives of Simancas, Spain, several years since and published in 1890 in Brown's Genesis of the United States, vol. I, page 190. This land is in the present town of Phippsburg. The description of Fort St. George gave it 12 pieces of ordnance, several houses, a church and a storehouse. Here was built the first vessel in America, the Virginia, 30 tons, the chief shipwright being one Digby of London. She carried the last of the colony back to England in 1608.

Col. Baldwin was Captain of a company in the expedition against Crown Point in 1755-56 and served in the same capacity from March to December, 1758, at Fort Ticonderoga and at Fort Du Quesne. The first portion of the Journal here printed is that kept by Capt. Baldwin at Fort William Henry, from December 1, 1755, to May 4, 1756. It is an interesting fact that twenty years after this he campaigned in the same section of country with Generals Schuyler, St. Clair and Gates, as Colonel and Chief of Engineers.

It is especially gratifying that The De Burians have had as editor of this volume and author of the Memoir of Col. Baldwin, his great-grandson, Mr. Thomas Williams Baldwin, who has devoted much painstaking care and a great deal of time to the preparation of the work. To him and to his sister, Miss Charlotte A. Baldwin, I wish to express my thanks for their great interest in placing this Journal before the historical students of the country. Moreover, I wish to make acknowledgement for the great assistance given in collating and revising the MS. for the press, to the other members of the Committee of Publication: Mr. Frank H. Damon and Bartlett Brooks, Esq.; also to Prof. James Brooks, a member of the Club, for his assistance in comparing the printer's copy with the original Journal.

As an important and interesting contribution to this subject, the Sermon delivered at the funeral of Col. Baldwin, by Rev. Daniel Foster, A. M., is reprinted from the exceedingly rare pamphlet printed at Worcester, Mass., by Edward E. Powars in 1789.

INTRODUCTION

And now, The De Burians of Bangor take pleasure in presenting this volume to that small number of collectors and libraries throughout the country, interested in preserving the details of our history, in which details posterity is said to delight.

For the Committee of Publication and for The De Burians,

SAMUEL LANE BOARDMAN,
President.

Bangor, Maine, October 20, 1906.

CONTENTS

	Page
DEDICATION	v
INTRODUCTION	vii
MEMOIR OF COL. BALDWIN	xiii
FUNERAL SERMON	xlv
REVOLUTIONARY JOURNAL	1
NOTES	143

PLATES

The Baldwin House		Frontispiece
Facsimile of Col. Baldwin's Letter to his Daughter	Page	xxxi
Grave of Col. Baldwin, North Brookfield, Mass.	"	xxxviii
Reproduction of Title-page of Funeral Sermon	"	xlvii
Facsimile of Page of Journal	"	81

MEMOIR OF COL. BALDWIN

MEMOIR

JEDUTHAN BALDWIN was born in Woburn, Mass., January 13, 1732. He lived here but a short time as his father, soon after his birth moved to Sudbury, Mass., but just what year we do not know.

In 1734 his father purchased land in Sudbury, his residence being given as of Woburn. In all later deeds his residence is given as of Sudbury, so probably it was in 1734 or shortly after that he took up his residence there.

He was the son of Isaac and Mary Flagg Baldwin, and grandson of Henry Baldwin of Woburn, who was the first of the family to settle in this country. His ancestors lived in what is now known as North Woburn, and built there in 1640 the house which has since always been and now is called The Baldwin House, an illustration of which forms the frontispiece to this volume.

It was a cousin of Jeduthan to whom we are indebted for the Baldwin apple. His cousin Loammi Baldwin, who served with distinction in the Revolutionary War, and who was said to have been with Washington on that winter night when he crossed the Delaware, was the originator of this apple. It is said that once, when making a survey at Wilmington, he observed some woodpeckers flying around a certain tree and going to it he found some excellent apples under it. He took from the tree scions which he grafted on to trees of his own. Subsequently when he attended Court in his capacity of High Sheriff, and also when he travelled anywhere, he was wont to take scions of this fruit, as well as the fruit itself, to distribute among his friends. At first these apples were called by some Butters apples, from the party on whose land the original apples were found, and by others Pecker apples from the bird that first drew attention to them. But it is said that one day when Col. Loammi Baldwin had a party of gentlemen to dine he set before them a dish of these apples, and they asked him by what name the apples were called. "By no name in particular," the Colonel replied; "call them, if you please, Baldwin apples." And this has been their name ever since. The original tree was blown down in the great gale of 1815.

Jeduthan Baldwin left Sudbury when quite young and settled in Brookfield, Mass. Just when he went there we do not know but we find that, on May 9, 1754, he purchased in Brookfield two lots of land, one of 6½ acres, and another of 16¼ acres. In these deeds his occupation is given as Housewright. In all subsequent deeds of land which he purchased, he is mentioned as Gentleman or the title Esq. is put after his name.

The town of Brookfield was divided into three precincts, one of which is now known as the town of North Brookfield. This was the part of the town in which he settled. He owned considerable land in the town during his life, as deeds are on record covering in the aggregate several hundred acres, which at different times he purchased, and but a small part of which he seems to have sold. The following item is taken from the report of the appraisers of his estate.

"The whole of the Real Estate, including the home farms, with the Buildings thereon standing, with a Pew in the Meeting House also one piece of Swamp and Meadow containing about 20 Acres, and another piece of Meadow containing three Acres, together with one-fourth part of the Brick Dwelling House formerly owned by Major Peter Harwood." This property the appraisers valued at 1085 pounds.

North Brookfield separated from the old town ecclesiastically in 1750, and educationally in 1756. And during the struggles of the eighteenth century this town took upon itself with the tacit consent of the mother town, the burden of paying its military expenses and furnishing its quota of soldiers for the wars.

In the spring of 1755 an expedition was planned against Crown Point, and Brookfield furnished her full quota for the expedition, Jeduthan being in command of a company, and we have his diary running from December, 1755, to May, 1756. Dr. Benj. Gott, who was surgeon's mate on the staff of Col. Josiah Brown and who remained at Fort William Henry till March 31, 1756 says in a petition: "I was at Fort William Henry last winter and know that Capt. Jeduthan Baldwin dealt out from his private stores, Rum, brandy, sugar, coffee, tea, wine, etc., to the sick in the Hospital, the Commissary being destitute."

Some time during this war Capt. Baldwin was wounded so severely in the leg that the council of surgeons declared it incurable and advised amputation. He protested against the measure but they insisted and were about to bind him and perform the operation when he raised himself in his bunk, seized his bayonet and threatened any one's life who should attempt to bind him, saying that if he went he would go altogether. Needless to say, that the operation was not performed and his leg was saved.

In 1757 Jeduthan Baldwin was married to Lucy, daughter of the Rev. Ebenezer Parkman of Westboro. Rev. Mr. Parkman was the first minister settled in Westboro, going there in 1724, and remaining until his death in 1782. When he was first in Westboro it was a long way into the wilds, and in his diary, which he kept and a considerable part of which is preserved in the Library of the American Antiquarian Society in Worcester, we get an interesting insight into the life of a minister in the pre-revolutionary times. In his diary under date of 1724 he tells of going to meeting with his pistol in his hand and being much frightened on his return by seeing what he supposed was an Indian approaching, but on coming nearer he found that it was his landlord. From the same source we learn that on August 20, 1756, Isaac Baldwin, (father of Jeduthan), called on Rev. Mr. Parkman and wife to ask their "approbation of his son Jeduthan proceedings with yr Dauter Lucy." The wedding day was afterwards set for April 21, 1757, but as the authorities appointed this day Fast Day Rev. Mr. Parkman sent word to Capt. Baldwin postponing the date of the wedding. By some chance the letter was not received and Capt. Baldwin did not learn of the postponement until his arrival in Westboro on the 20th. The wedding was solemnized on April 28th, under which date we find the following entry in the diary:

"Capt. Baldwin Came, accopanyd by his Br Nahum, but his Father & Mother whom I had writ to came not. My son Thomas went to Mr. Stowe of Southb. & brot up

Miss Huldah. p. m. Mr. Martyn & his wife came. My son Ebr & his wife, at eve Mr. John Martyn junior & his wife and at ye edge of even'g the marriage of my Dauter Lucy was solemnized by Rev. Mr. Martyn."

Under date of May 2, we find the following entry: "Cold. Capt. Baldwin left us to go to Brookfield to come again not till after election. Miss Huldah still with us, a sober discreet young lady assists Lucy in Quilting a Bed Quilt."

Mrs. Baldwin remained with her father for a month after the wedding, and then Capt. Baldwin came and took her home to Brookfield. In Rev. Mr. Parkman's diary under date of June 8 we read that: "Capt. Baldwin (wo came a little after midnight) to day takes his wife out in a Chair and yy ride over to Mr. Martyns and return at eve'g p. m. came his Father & Mother; & at ev'g his Uncle Saml. (with whom he served apprenticeship) yy supped & lodg'd here. I wd view ye kind Hand of Prov. yt wl I was somewt put to't for fresh meat, Mr. Maynd kindly sent me a Qr of veal & some Butter, Mrs. Dolly Rice an old Cheese. Thos. went to Southboro to invite Miss Huldah Stow to go with his sister to Brookfield, but returned without her, it being too short warning, yet longer cd not be given her. Lucy was so ill yesterday yt it was uncertain whether she cd go herself."

Under date of June 9 he says: "Still hot and dry. My Dauter Lucy left us, & went with her husband to Brookfield. The Company yt went from home with them were his Father & Mother & Uncle Samuel Baldwin."

In the part of Rev. Mr. Parkman's diary covering the years 1756 to 1761 frequent mention is made of Capt. Baldwin, who on his way to Boston or elsewhere, would tarry for a day or night with his father in law.

Capt. Jeduthan Baldwin was in military service throughout the French and Indian war and we find it recorded that he was in service from March to December, 1759, and we find references to him in Commissary Wilson's Orderly Book, at the expedition of the British and Provincial Army under Maj. Gen. Jaffrey Amherst against Ticonderoga and Crown Point, 1759.

In March, 1759, Capt. Baldwin's father died and we find in the Diary the following entries:

"13. Wn I came home rec. a Letter from my Son Baldwin to inform me yt his Father Baldwin dyd yesterday morning and to desire me to go to ye Funeral to morrow."

"14. The morning was very stormy snowd & blowd so yt I soon gave up all Thoughts of going to ye Funeral of Br Baldwin neither cd I so much as go to Southboro where I had designed before I recd ye Letter of my Son Baldwin."

After the war Capt. Baldwin went into trading as is shown by the following entries in Rev. Mr. Parkman's diary.

"Nov. 14, 1760. My Son Baldwin from Boston here is going home with Quantity of goods in his carts, being abt to set up Trading."

And again under date of February 4, 1761: "Billy set out for Boston in his Master Baldwin's Service."

"Feb. 7 a very rainy Time, yet at eve'g Billy returned from Boston having loaded up Mr. Walcott, as well as Mr. Bartlett's waggons from Brookfield for his Br Baldwin."

"Feb. 20. At night in ye Rain comes my son Baldwin & a negro he has bought of Maj. Curtis of Sudbury, a Chair & 2 Horses so yt he has here at my Barn three Horses."

"21. A Rainy morning abt 10 cleared. My Baldwins & their Negro Set out on their journey afterward it rains again & I fear they will not get home."

From this time to the opening of the Revolutionary contest we have no knowledge of his movements but we infer that he prospered in his undertakings for during this period we find he bought several parcels of land in Brookfield and was quite a land owner at the time of the opening of the Revolution.

It was during this period that he came into possession of a clock, the case of which he is reported to have made himself. The face of the clock bears the inscription "Jedu Baldwin Brookfield 1766." It not only tells the time of day, but also the day of the month. The works are of brass and are said to have come from England. The clock is today in good condition and keeping accurate time at the residence of Miss Charlotte A. Baldwin in Bangor, Maine.

From a Bi-Centennial Oration delivered at West Brookfield, July 4, 1860, by Lyman Whiting, D. D., we learn that on December 7, 1773 a meeting of the citizens of the town was held and two letters were read from the town of Boston. At this meeting a committee of five, of which Capt. Baldwin was one, was appointed to consider and report a proper resolve relating to the importation of tea from Great Britain, "and such other matters as are proper for this town to do at this difficult time." This Committee made the following report with accompanying resolve:

"We think it our indispensable duty, in the most public manner to let the world know our utter abhorrence of the last and most detestable scheme, in the introduction of Tea from Great Britain to be peddled out amongst us, by which means we were to be made to swallow a poison more fatal in its effects to the national and political Rights and Privileges of the People of this country, than ratsbane would be to the natural body.

"Therefore, Resolved, that we will not by any way or means knowingly encourage or promote the sale or consumption of any Tea whatever, subject to a duty payable in America, but all persons whoever they may be, who shall be concerned in a transaction so dangerous, shall be held by us in the utmost contempt, and be deemed enemies to the well being of this country."

The authority above mentioned also gives the following sentences from the report of this committee:

"Loyalty and fidelity to our most gracious King, George the Third, and due obedience to the government under him, by Divine Providence and by Law established in this Province, we will to the utmost of our power maintain and defend. An uninterrupted Friendship and Commerce with the Country of our Father's nativity, we wish to continue to our latest Generation; but our dear bought rights and privileges we will never tamely give up." Further on they say "of our dearest civil and religious privileges when wrested from us, we shall not think our lives and property too much to be spent in their defence and recovery."

At a Town Meeting held March 14, 1774, Capt. Jeduthan Baldwin was chosen Town Clerk; also elected one of the Board of five Selectmen; also one of two surveyors of shingles.

September 12, 1774, a Committee of Correspondence consisting of eleven members was chosen by the Town and Capt. Baldwin served on this Committee.

September 26, 1774, Jedidiah Foster Esq., Capt. Jeduthan Baldwin and Phineas Upham were chosen delegates to the Provincial Congress to be held at Concord. This Congress met in Salem on Friday, October 7, 1774, and at once adjourned to meet at the Meeting House in Concord. They met here for a week and then adjourned to Cambridge. This Congress was in session till October 29th, and then adjourned to November 23. When they met in November it seems to have been difficult to secure the attendance of the members for on the journal of the Congress under date of Friday, November 25th, we find the following resolve:

"Resolved, that Doct'r Holton, Doct'r Foster, Col. Roberson, Capt. Baldwin and Mr. Cushing be a Committee to wait on such Gentlemen of his Majesties Constitutional Council of this province, who are now in Town at the request of this Congress, and acquaint them, that this Congress respectfully acknowledge their cheerful attendance but will not be ready to offer any matters for their advice, until a Quorum of that Hon. Board shall appear, and which is soon expected, and that in the meantime a seat is provided for them in this House if they shall see cause to be present."

This is the only Committee on which we find the name of Capt. Baldwin. This Committee did not meet with much success for on the following day they reported that they had found but two of the absent members in town but had delivered them the message. The Committee were then ordered "to wait on the other Gentlemen of his Majesty's Council invited by this Congress to attend here as they come to Town and inform them of the Resolve of this Congress."

This Congress finally adjourned December 10, 1774. It was presided over by the Hon. John Hancock.

At a meeting of the Town held on December 26, 1774, a vote was passed to allow Jeduthan Baldwin £9-14 for services as delegate to the Provincial Congress at Concord and Cambridge, 45 days.

In January, 1775, a meeting was held and it was "Voted That the ministers be desired to notify contributions for the Boston sufferers." A committee of three, one from each precinct, was chosen to receive these contributions and transport them to Boston. Jeduthan Baldwin was the member from the Second Precinct or North Brookfield.

We know not what success the committee as a whole had, but we find in Vol. 4 of the Fourth Series of the Massachusetts Historical Collections the following letter which shows what success crowned the efforts of Capt. Baldwin:

"BROOKFIELD, February 6, 1775.
"TO THE COMMITTEE OF DONATIONS,
  "GENTLEMEN,
    "The bearer, Mr. Ayres, will deliver you 30 bushels rye, 14 do. Indian corn, ½ bushel beans, and 18 cheeses, weight 224 lbs., and two dollars in cash, which I received of the inhabitants of the second precinct in Brookfield, for the suffering poor of Boston, and is the whole that is brought in. There is not a man in this place but wishes you success, and are ready to lend you their assistance to the last extremity.
  " I am your very humble servant,
    "JEDU. BALDWIN, Committee."

In reply a letter was sent, which was a copy of a letter sent to the town of Brookline and which is printed in the collection above referred to. In this letter the committee acknowledge receipt of the contributions and thank the citizens for their generous donation to the people of Boston, "who are now suffering the severity of ministerial vengeance, for nobly exerting themselves in the glorious cause of American liberty. We trust that by the blessing of Heaven, and the kind assistance of our sympathizing and benevolent brethren, in this and the other Colonies, we shall be enabled to stand firm (as we have hitherto done), to the disappointment and disgrace of the enemies of America and the liberties of mankind. Accept of our grateful thanks for this mark of your affection and sympathy towards us in our unhappy situation.

"I am with due acknowledgments for the care you have taken, in the name of the Committee, Gentlemen,

"Your obliged friend and servant,

"THOMAS CRAFTS, Jun."

In 1775 Capt. Baldwin was again at his service with the army as the following letter, the original of which is preserved in the library of the American Antiquarian Society at Worcester, will testify:

"CAMP AT PROSPECT HILL, July 7, 1775.

"DEAR SIR: Last evening I had the pleasure of hearing of your return to Brookfield, by Mr. Sullivan, who informed me that matters were settled agreeably at Ticonderoga, and that the fort was under good circumstances, after meeting with some opposition with one of the officers. By an invitation from Col. Gridley, I went as an engineer (the 16th of June) upon Bunker Hill, in Charlestown, and threw up a breastwork, and was on that hill the whole of that memorable day. Ye 17th of June, at evening, we retreated out to Prospect Hill, and worked again all that night throwing up breastworks; and I have continued in that service as an engineer to this time.

I propose to stay here about a fortnight; by that time I expect to finish the fortification on this hill, and then I expect to return home, as there is no provision made for me in the army, and the Congress are requested by Gen. Washington not to give out any more commissions. You proposed to me to have another Member chosen to represent Brookfield with you. It would be very agreeable to me to have the favour of the people.

"I am, Sir, your very humble servant,
"JEDU'N BALDWIN."

At Bunker Hill his brother Isaac was killed. Isaac Baldwin at the very commencement of the war raised a company of men in Hillsborough, N. H., and brought them to Cambridge. While there with his men a tender belonging to the enemy got aground on the Chelsea ferry ways and he went with twelve of his men in open day in the face of the enemy and burned her, after taking out her guns and sails, by throwing a pitchfork of hay on fire in the cabin windows. Having accomplished this he put his men back one by one and himself brought up the rear under the fire of the British fleet and in this way reached their quarters safely with four of his men wounded. He fought valiantly at Bunker Hill and was shot through the breast and died that night. He is said to have loaded and discharged his musket three times after he was wounded.

When his men were carrying him off the field he exhorted them to fight saying "that they would win the day, and he would be with them again directly." He died that night.

Jeduthan Baldwin was active in planning the work around Boston during its investment and on March 17, 1776, he was made assistant engineer with rank of Captain at Cambridge. The diary of his which is here published commences December 8, 1775, and shows him to have been at Cambridge and vicinity until the middle of March, 1776, when he received orders to go to New York, where he was set at work on the fortifications. April 26, 1776, he was placed on the continental establishment with rank and pay of Lieut. Colonel, and ordered to Canada. He went up the Hudson to Albany and by way of Fort Edward and Ticonderoga and down the river Sorell to Shambalee and Sorell. Here he met the army retreating. By the last of July he was back at Ticonderoga and was there at the time of Burgoyne's surrender. September 3, 1776, he was made engineer with the rank of colonel. In December, 1776, he returned to his home in Brookfield and in January, 1777, went to Boston and Portsmouth, N. H., but by the first of February he was back at Albany on his way to Lake George. He remained at Lake George until November when he again returned home. He served under Gen. St. Clair at Ticonderoga this year. For the next six months we have not his diary, but in July of that year he was in the neighborhood of New York, where he remained the rest of the year. This is as far as this diary goes but the diary of Rev. Ebenezer Parkman for the years 1779 and 1780 has been published and from this we get occasional glimpses of Col. Baldwin, and learn something of his movements.

In his diary under date of March 14, 1776, he speaks of dining with Mr. Samuel Baldwin at Roxbury. This was Rev. Samuel Baldwin, who was a cousin of his and a Presbyterian clergyman, of whom it is said that he used to carry his arms to church, and on Thanksgiving Day, 1775, when addressing the Throne of Grace he thanked the Lord " that there was sufficient hemp in the colonies to hang all the Tories."

It was while at Ticonderoga in 1776 that he wrote a letter to his daughter Betsey which fortunately has been preserved; a fac simile reproduction of which is given on the opposite page.

In a book privately issued by the Massachusetts Chapters of the Daughters of the Revolution, and which is entitled: Honor Roll of Massachusetts Patriots Heretofore Unknown, and which contains a list of men and women who loaned money to the Government during the years 1777–1779, I find the name of Zeduthun Baldwin, which is probably meant for Jeduthan Baldwin, although in the list his residence is given as Lancaster instead of Brookfield.

By Resolve of Congress of March 11, 1779, a Corps of Engineers was formed with three companies of Sappers and Miners, which a Resolve of date of May 27, 1778, had ordered to be raised, all of them to be under the direction of the Chief Engineer.

It is interesting to note that this Corps was officered almost entirely by Frenchmen, there being but two or possibly three Americans in its list of officers.

The following were the officers who served in this Corps, as given in Heitman's Historical Register of Officers of the Continental Army, and Hamersly's Army and Navy Register:

Chief Engineer: Brigadier General Louis Lebique Duportail.

Colonel Thaddeus Kosciusko
Colonel Baileul de la Radiere
Colonel —— de Laumoy
Lieutenant Colonel Cheval de Cambray
Major Jean Baptiste Obrey de Gouvion
Major Cheval de Villefranche
Major John Barnard de Murnan
Captain Pierre Charles L'Enfant
Captain Joseph Detzon
Captain Daniel Nevin

Colonel Jeduthun Baldwin
Major Ferdinand de Brahm

Rev. Mr. Parkman seems to have shared in common with many others at that time the antipathy against Masonry, for under date of May 25 and 26, 1780, we find the following entries in his diary:

"May 25 I found that my son Breck is a FREE MASON."

"26 I discover also that my son Sam is, that Capt. Elias and yt Col. Baldwin are."

We do not know to what lodge Col. Baldwin belonged, having found nothing that would give us information on this point. The only other information we have as to his being a Mason is found in his diary under date of Nov. 4, 1777, where he says: "admitted to an Honble Assembly." And again on Nov. 12 he says: "Recd into a Society as a Craftsman." We understand that there were many lodges formed in the army and possibly it was to one of these that he belonged.

During the year 1780 we find from a Memorandum Book kept by Ebenezer Parkman, Jr., who was with the Revolutionary Army, that Col. Baldwin was during the early part of the year at Morristown, N. J., and in February went to Philadelphia, where he remained a month and then returned to Morristown, going home to Brookfield in June for a few months. In the Fall of 1780 he was at West Point with his regiment of artificers. He resigned on April 26, 1782.

It is reported that it was a member of Col. Baldwin's regiment who made the coffin that Major Andre was buried in.

Just before the army of the American Revolution was disbanded, at the suggestion of Gen. Knox, the officers formed themselves in April 1783 into a secret society for the purpose of keeping up their friendly intercourse and keeping fresh the heroic memories of the struggle they had been through. They likened themselves to Cincinnatus, who left his plow to lead an army and returned, after his war duties were over, to the plow again. Hence they called themselves The Society of The Cincinnati. They adopted a constitution and formed by-laws and chose Gen. Washington as their first President. Its branches in the several States were to hold meetings each Fourth of July and the general society to hold a meeting every May. The order was to be kept alive by descent through the eldest male representative of the members of the families. In its main intent the Society was to be a kind of masonic brotherhood charged with the duty of aiding the widows and orphans of its members in time of need. The autograph list of the original members of the Massachusetts Society, deposited in the safety vault of the New England Historic-Genealogical Society, contains the names of 320 officers and among them is found the name of Col. Jeduthan Baldwin.

In March, 1784, an academy was organized at Leicester, Mass., and in 1786 Col. Baldwin was a contributor to a fund for the academy to the amount of one hundred pounds.

In a Brief Sketch of the History of Leicester Academy, published by Emory Washburn in 1855, we find a notice of Col. Baldwin which in part is as follows:

"Col. Jeduthan Baldwin deserves a prominent place in these notices on many accounts.

"He became a contributor to the fund in the sum above stated, in 1786, to enable the institution to struggle with the embarassments that grew more oppressive, as the currency of the country depreciated, and the general stagnation of business paralyzed the industry of the citizen. For this generous and opportune assistance, the trustees passed a vote of thanks, May 23rd, 1787.

"Colonel Baldwin belonged to Brookfield. He was born in 1731, and died June 4th, 1788. A sermon, commemorative of his character, was preached by the Rev. Mr. Foster, of New Braintree, which was published.

"He held, for many years, a prominent station in public life. As a military man, his reputation was distinguished. In the French war, at an early age, he held the commission of captain.

"He took an active part in the measures of the Revolution, and was a member of the first Provincial Congress that convened in October, 1774. Its records shew that he took a prominent part in its proceedings.

"He was, moreover, a member of the convention of the committees of correspondence that met at Worcester, in August, 1774, being associated with Judge Jedediah Foster and Capt. Phinehas Upham on that occasion.

"The importance of these trusts will be understood when it is remembered that, to these congresses and conventions, the government of the province was practically committed for several months after October, 1774, during which time the opposition to the mother country was assuming its form and consistency.

"He early took part, as a military man, in the revolutionary struggle, and, upon the organization of the continental forces, was promoted to the rank of Colonel, in which, it is said, "his conduct procured for him the cooperation of the first characters, and received the general approbation and esteem of his fellow soldiers and citizens."

"Surely his name should be held in grateful remembrance by Leicester Academy for his friendship to her in her weakness and, in a sketch of her history, he deservedly holds a place."

In 1787 what is known as Shay's Rebellion broke out and the inhabitants of North Brookfield were interested spectators, for this Daniel Shay who was at the head of the rebellion was for a time a resident of Brookfield and in 1772 married Abigail Gilbert of that town. While he had many recruits from this section yet prompt and effective aid was rendered the government. Besides a company of infantry from the South Parish and a part of Col. Crafts company of cavalry, there was also a company of volunteers from the town under the command of Col. Jeduthan Baldwin. This company joined to Col. Crafts and conveyed in sleighs did effective work. They were sent to a place called Murrayfield to cut off a supply of provisions destined for the aid of Shay, which was guarded by a detail of soldiers. By making a sudden attack on the place at midnight they captured the whole party with fourteen sleigh loads of provisions, and the next day they pursued and routed what was left of Shay's band. We have preserved a memorandum giving the testimony or a part of it taken at the trial of the insurgents, which was kept by Col. Baldwin.

At a town meeting in Brookfield held December 26, 1786, a Report was adopted and forwarded to the Governor praying for an Act of indemnity in favor of the Insurgents, and this was followed about a month later by a Protest signed by ninety-six of the inhabitants of the town.

Col. Baldwin died at North Brookfield June 4, 1788, and on his tombstone we find the following inscription:

> Be it remembered
> that
> Here lies the Body of
> Jeduthun Baldwin Esq.
> Col & Engineer in the late
> American war
> Who died June the 4th 1788
> Aged 56
> He was a true Patriot
> an intripid soldier
> an exemplary Christian
> and a friend to all mankind
> Blessed are the dead who die in the Lord

The North Brookfield minister being absent his funeral sermon was preached by the Rev. Daniel Foster A. M. from the neighboring town of New Braintree. The sermon was printed in Worcester in 1789 by Edward E. Powars, and I have been fortunate enough to find a copy of it.

The title page of the sermon is as follows:

Consolation in Adversity and Hope in Death. A Sermon Preached at the Funeral of Jeduthan Baldwin Esq. At Brookfield, June 6th, 1788, Who Died June 4th, aetat. 57. By Daniel Foster, A. M. Pastor of the Church in New Braintree.

GRAVE OF COL. JEDUTHAN BALDWIN, NORTH BROOKFIELD, MASS.

"Thy dead men shall live; together with my dead body, shall they arise: awake and sing, ye that dwelt in the dust; for thy dew is as the dew of herbs, and the earth shall cast out the dead."

PROPHET ISAIAH.

"Wherefore comfort one another with these words."

ST. PAUL.

The sermon also bears the following dedication:

"To Mrs. Lucy Baldwin, Bereaved Relict of Jeduthan Baldwin, Esquire, and to his surviving Son and Daughter, this Sermon delivered at his Funeral, and now by their desire published, is respectfully inscribed, by their sympathizing friend, The Author."

Besides the two children mentioned in the dedication, he had two other children, one of whom, Jeduthan, was killed by being thrown from a cart October 31, 1763, in the 6th year of his age. In the sermon he is spoken of as "in an instant flung out of time into eternity." The other child was Isaac who died April 1st, 1783, aged 19. A foot note to one of the pages of the sermon says of him; "He was a senior sophister in the University of Cambridge, a youth of an amiable disposition, studious and exemplary, greatly beloved by all his acquaintance while living, and much lamented now dead."

The surviving son above referred to was Luke Baldwin concerning whom we find the following entry in the diary of Rev. E. Parkman under date of Sept. 13, 1779:

"Luke Baldwin from Brookfield and lodges, a pretty, agreeable, hopeful lad. May God make him a great Blessing."

Luke afterwards moved to the West Parish where the book of records kept in the Library building at North Brookfield says he built a magnificent house. Early in the nineteenth century he went to Boston to live, where he remained until his death in 1832. He left a large family and one of his sons, Thomas W. moved to Bangor, Maine, in 1837, and resided there until his death in 1874. He was the father of the editor of this volume.

We think we cannot close this Memoir better than by giving the following obituary notice, which appeared in the Massachusetts Spy, a newspaper published in Worcester under date of June 19, 1788:

"*Brookfield, June 11th, 1788.*

"Died in this town, on the 4th day of June inst. Jeduthan Baldwin, Esq.; in the 57th year of his age; and on the Friday following his remains were decently interred, in the presence of a large concourse of his friends and neighbours, who assembled on that sorrowful occasion to pay their last tribute of affection and esteem to a *worthy man;* at which time (the Clergymen of the town of Brookfield being absent) a pathetick and well adapted discourse was delivered, in the north parish meeting house, by the *Rev. Daniel Foster* of New Braintree, from Job xiv 10.—*But man dieth and wasteth away; yea, man giveth up the ghost, and where is he?*

"Such are the feelings of the human heart, that when a good man is arrested by the cold hand of death, and laid in the silent mansion of the dead, his friends forget his foibles, and his enemies, unless they are more cruel than the grave, cannot but remember his virtues. When an intimate friend and a pleasant companion is taken from our arms, and shut out from our society, we may be too apt to be partial in a description of his merits; Hence it is, that so little regard is often with propriety had to the descriptions of this kind on such occasions. Idle then would be the hope of raising a man's character in the eye of the world by painting his accomplishments in lively colours. Happy are they who need not the pen of an ingenious composuist to perpetuate their memory—whose life has impressed on the minds of all who knew them, an indelible remembrance of a good name. Yet, to be silent on the departure of a man of uncommon worth, though it might not affect the memory of the deceased, would discover a too careless attention to *virtue itself.*

"Col. Baldwin, from his youth, has ever discovered himself to be a man of ingenuity, firmness and fidelity, in whatever office or employment he has been engaged. In the early part of his life he proved himself a friend to his country, and a faithful subject to the government under which he was born, by risking his life in its defence against the French; in which war, raised by his merit, though a youth, he was honoured with a Captain's commission. Early in the contest between Great Britain and the United States, he discovered himself a friend to the *rights of humanity*, and an unshaken advocate for the liberties of America. On the first alarm of war, when danger invaded his country, he drew his sword in its defence, nor did he return it to its sheath until he saw an accomplishment of his wishes in the establishment of the freedom and independence of the United States. His conduct as a Colonel in the continental army during the war procured him the confidence of the first characters, and secured the general approbation and esteem of his fellow soldiers and citizens. He cheerfully endured the hardships of the camp and the fatigues of war, in the pleasing hope, that America, by the patriotick exertions of her sons, would become an asylum for the opprest, and the delightful land of freedom and felicity; — in this hope he has ever stood ready to step forth and resist every measure which he conceived had a tendency to blast these pleasing prospects. But alas! just as these beautiful scenes are opening—while his fellow citizens are rejoicing in the expectation of a speedy establishment of liberty and national prosperity—in the midst of his days, he is cut off, and his eyes are closed from terrestrial scenes! But though he has not lived to share the rewards due to his merit in this world, his friends may console themselves in the full persuasion, that his posterity shall inherit the blessings for which he fought, and that he himself, in a better world, shall be adorned with unfading laurels—for Col. Baldwin was not only a soldier and a patriot, but he was a christian; free from that bigotry and contractedness of mind which too often blemishes the character of the serious and devout followers of the Saviour of Mankind, he was a strict and careful observer of the principles of christianity; he was liberal in his sentiments, and his life was exemplary; his mind was clear and candid; he was cool and deliberate in forming his resolutions, open and frank in declaring them, and steady and persevering in the carrying them into effect; his judgement was ever the most esteemed and regarded by those who had the pleasure of being the best acquainted with him; though agreeable in his manners, and manly in his address, yet a slight acquaintance was insufficient to discover his real worth; the virtues in which he most excelled were those which most adorn the human mind—in the *social virtues* he shone with peculiar lustre; his house was the mansion of hospitality—he was a pleasant companion—an affectionate husband—an indulgent parent—and a faithful friend;—he was a man of *sensibility*— he had a *feeling heart*, and a *friendly hand*—even the tongue of envy dare not but say, *the virtues of humanity were his*—then let his enemies tread lightly on the *turf* and let his friends, with sympathetick tears, bedew the *sods* that cover *the poor mans friend.*"

Since writing this Memoir announcement has been made by the War Department that the new Fort at the mouth of the Kennebec River, Maine, is named Fort Baldwin in honor and recognition of the services rendered in the War of the Revolution by Col. Jeduthan Baldwin. This was brought about through the efforts of Col. John H. Calef, U. S. A., retired, who is a descendant of Col. Baldwin and has been earnest in his endeavors to have such recognition made.

FUNERAL SERMON

CONSOLATION IN ADVERSITY,
AND
HOPE IN DEATH.

A
SERMON,
PREACHED AT THE
FUNERAL
OF
JEDUTHAN BALDWIN, Esq.
AT BROOKFIELD, JUNE 6th, 1788.
WHO DIED JUNE 4th, Ætat. 57.

BY DANIEL FOSTER, A. M.
PASTOR OF THE CHURCH IN NEW-BRAINTREE.

"Thy dead men shall live; together with my dead body, shall they arise: awake and sing, ye that dwell in the dust; for thy dew is as the dew of herbs, and the earth shall cast out the dead."   PROPHET ISAIAH.
"Wherefore comfort one another with these words."
                                ST. PAUL.

COMMONWEATH OF MASSACHUSETTS:
WORCESTER: PRINTED BY EDWARD E. POWARS.
M,DCC,LXXXIX.

FACSIMILE OF TITLE PAGE OF FUNERAL SERMON

FUNERAL SERMON

JOB xiv. 10.

"But MAN dieth, and wasteth away; yea, Man giveth up the ghosth, and where is he?"—

THE providence that has called us together this day, is truly solemn and interesting; and the scene portrayed before our eyes, gloomy and affecting — Not much unlike that which caused the SAVIOUR of the world, when he stood amidst weeping friends at the grave, to drop a tear — We have consigned to the silent grave, 'till the heavens are no more, the wasted remains of our Friend and Brother — And are come now to the house of GOD, like the disciples of John, to tell JESUS.

In this chapter, there is a most melancholly account of human nature — Few are the days of man upon earth, and they are filled up with anxiety and trouble. There is a pathetick prayer in the vi. verse, That GOD would turn away his afflicting hand from *him*, that he may have some present ease and comfort; or, that he might cease to live, and find that longed-for point of time, when he should be dismissed from sorrow, and introduced to a better world. In the vii. verse, he is compared to a tree, and his condition considered to be more hopeless than the trees that are cut down; if it were not for another life and world.

But man dieth, is weakened, or cut off; yea, man giveth up the ghost, or spirit, and where is he?

He, who was endued with reason and understanding, memory and judgement; who was capable of reflecting upon his own actions, and contemplating the works of the DEITY; he who was the Husband, the Father, the Friend, conversant with us a few days ago, and animated with the same hopes, and filled with the same fears that we now are—*where is he?*

We have, in the text, with its connection, expressed the state and condition of man in this world, represented as a state of disappointment and trouble:—His end, or departure out of it—he dieth and wasteth away;—

And a strong implication that he is somewhere in the dominions of JEHOVAH, has still a conscious existence, and his spirit is with the FATHER OF SPIRITS—He giveth up the ghost, and where is he?

1. The state and condition of man in this world is represented as a state of disappointment and trouble.

Since sin has stained and tarnished the beauty of this

lower creation, debased and degraded the noble nature of man, this life is little else than a scene of sorrow and inconvenience.

The Apostle informs us of the entrance of sin into the world, and the dire train of evils that hover round the human race, in consequence thereof.

Indeed, every part of the universe feels the sad effects of the original apostacy; and no part more than the body and mind of man.—"*In Adam all die.*"

The story of man, is a short and pitiful one indeed.—Ask thy father, and he will tell thee—Go with me to the Egyptian coast, and hear Pharoah question the patriarch Jacob—"*How old art thou?*" See the venerable old man rise and bow to the king, and hear the simple and affecting story of his life—"*Few, and evil, have the days of the years of my life been.*"

We are born with pain and trouble to our parents, and inconvenience to ourselves; and a great part of our time in this world is past before we arrive to years fit for moral and religious improvements.

How anxious and uneasy are youth, in climbing the hill of life, and eager in grasping after the phantom, HAPPINESS; 'till some sad disappointment, some alarming providence, reduces them to a just sense of things. And no sooner do we arrive at manhood, the meridian of our days, than new and unexpected scenes of trouble open upon us.

The husband is called to administer to the wife of his youth, in the agonies of death:—At the same time, endeavouring to calm the breasts of his little distressed family, till the eloquent sigh, the expressive throb, the insensible tear prevent.

The wife, in her turn, to close the eyes of her beloved husband, the joy of her heart, and comfort of her days.—The knot of sympathy and friendship is untied by the cruel hand of death—clusters of woes break in upon her, and her grief is insupportable!—O, my fatherless children, who will care for you in this unrelenting world.—I will go mourning all my days, 'till kind death close the scene of grief.

Sometimes the happy, the afflicted pair, walk hand in hand, to the silent grave, after a darling son, whom they said should comfort them concerning the work of their hands, close their eyes, and inherit their substance. And children, often, by their sin, and undutifulness to their parents cause the greatest grief, yea, bring their gray hairs, with sorrow, down to the grave. And parents, by their folly and vanity, cause pious children to tremble at the scene that death is ready to open upon them.

If we add to these, the fear of greater evils, that of death in special, we shall be induced to say—"*Man that is born of a woman, is of few days, and full of trouble.*"

There are, besides these, calamities common to all men,

particular afflictions, those have, who live godly in CHRIST JESUS.

True Christians have great trials and troubles, arising from a sense of their ignorance, imperfection and sin.—Yea, this is the greatest burden of their lives.—They often pray with David—"*Create in me a clean heart*"—weep with Peter, when they have, in any instances been left, practically, to deny CHRIST;—and groan with the Apostle, "*O, wretched man that I am!*"

Wicked men likewise, add to the miseries of life, evils, of which they have no comfortable hope, there will be a redress at death. When they sacrifice the rights of conscience, violate God's holy law, drown their reason by intemperance, polute their bodies by debauchery, break marriage vows, betray virgin innocency; and live in neglect of the great Salvation, their consciences read them lectures of shame, remorse and horror.—The thought of death, fills them with a chilling fear.—"*They travel in pain all their days, a dreadful sound is in their ears, in prosperity the destroyer cometh* upon them."

And when men have, with pain and trouble, travelled the tiresome journey of life, 'til they come to the close.

2. Their departure is gloomy—'Tis so on account of what takes place before, and likewise what follows after.

Pain, uneasiness, and old age, are often the herbingers of death, and proclaim that a dissolution is at hand.—

Under these, they groan, being burdened, "*Let me alone for my days are vanity.*" The little the best of men know, in this life, of the enjoyments and employments of the world to come, increases the pain of dying.

The doubts and fears, likewise, that cloud their minds, concerning their preparedness to leave the world, are no small ingredients in the sorrows of a death-bed! "*Not that I would be unclothed* saith the Apostle, *but clothed upon.*" And the same Apostle tells us of those, "*who through fear of death, were all their life time subject to bondage.*" The light which we have by the coming and death of CHRIST, and the glorious declarations of the Gospel, concerning another world, are great and animating; but they do not entirely dispel the horror, and scatter the gloom that hang over death and the grave.

When we waste away and die, there is likewise occasion given to the living of sorrow and grief, tears are a tribute due to the dead, "*because man goeth to his long home, the mourners go about the streets.*" GOD has ever tolerated mourning for the dead. The whole congregation of Israel mourned for Moses and Aaron, and when the man of GOD was dead, the Prophet took up his carcass and laid it in his own grave, "and they mourned over him, saying, alas, my brother." And under the present dispensation, we find, "devout men carried Stephen to his burial, and made great lamentation over him."

And our BLESSED LORD set us the example at the grave of Lazarus his friend.

It is solemn to die likewise, for after death, "THE JUDGEMENT." The judgement that men pass upon their actions in this world, when their passions run in their own proper channel, is a prelude to the judgement of GOD! Scripture, reason, and the unequal distributions of rewards and punishments in this world, declare for a judgement to come, and strenuously implead the doctrine of an intermediate space between the death of the body, and the rewards and punishments of the life to come.

But 3. We are taught in the text, that man has still a conscious existence, and his spirit is with the Father of Spirits.

Man is made up of two constituent parts, body and soul. His body was taken from the earth, but his soul came from heaven. This is the account Divine Revelation gives, in addition to the law and light of nature. "*And the LORD GOD formed man of the dust of the ground, and breathed into his nostrils the breath of life, and man became a living soul.*" The body was curiously formed by the finger of GOD; but his spirit, the immortal inhabitant, came immediately from GOD.

"There is a spirit in man, says Elihu, and the inspiration of the Almighty giveth them understanding."

The sacred pages inform us also, what will take place at death, the body dieth and wasteth away, and the spirit is given up. "*Then shall the dust return to the dust as it was, and the spirit to GOD who gave it.*" GOD has been giving intimations of another life and world in different dispensations, from the morning of time down to this day. Before the giving of the law, He took that eminent Prophet and faithful preacher of righteousness, Enoch, from this sinful world to his heavenly habitation; which was an evidence to the men of that generation, of another life, of the care GOD took of the bodies of his people, and of a resurrection.

Under the law, to revive the sense of another world, and the resurrection of the body GOD sent a convoy of angels to conduct the prophet Elijah from this guilty globe to more noble employments in the upper world— "*And Elijah went up by a whirlwind into heaven.*" And under this dispensation, the greatest that was ever born of a woman, was put to death in the flesh—JESUS, the Resurrection and the Life, visited the tomb, and explored the silent mansions of the dead; but this Prisoner proved too mighty for the King of Terrors; on the third day he revived, he burst asunder the marble bars of death, came forth, and shewed himself the very CHRIST.

Now there is a new face put upon GOD'S economy with mankind; and the darkness and uncertainty that hung over the person; the doctrines of the SAVIOUR, and the world to come, are removed: He has bought the grave, it is no longer a prison, but a house, yea, his inner chamber, here the saints of the Most High God may rest in hope, till the last grand revolution. When he, who in his humiliation wore a crown of thorns, and by his sufferings, procured the keys of death and hell, shall come in the clouds of heaven, with a crown the resplendent rays of which shall dash out yonder sun, and quench all the lamp of heaven, accompanied with the archangel, and the trump of God; whose blast shall awake their slumbers and reanimate their dust: Then *"that which was sown in dishonor, shall be raised in power,"* and that saying brought to pass, *"O grave I will be thy destruction."*

Here, christian friends, is consolation under all the pressures of time, and a balance for the inconveniences of this world; Here is hope for the children of God, by regeneration, in the hour of death; and from hence we may draw our comfort concerning our friends who have fallen asleep in Jesus—*"Wherefore comfort one another with these words."*

Permit me to subjoin a few reflections.

1. What we have heard, should teach us a lesson of humility and submission. It is for sin, that God inflicts all these natural evils upon us; and his design is to induce us to hate sin, wean us from this world, and attach us to

a better. Here we are in a state of trial and probation, training up for another life; and it does not become us to repine and grieve at the evils that befall us here; they may be productive of our happiness through the whole term of our existence.

2. We should not be over-awed at the appearance of death: It will free us from all the sorrows, pains, disappointments and sufferings of this life, and introduce us into joys unspeakable and full of glory: Our bodies will rest quietly in the grave, with "kings and counsellors of the earth, who built desolate places for themselves," and our spirits will join the general assembly and church of the first born in heaven, where we shall have no painful remembrance of the wormwood and the gall, that were given us to drink in this world!

3. We should take comfort concerning our friends who sleep in Jesus. All that death has done, is to change the mode of their existence:—From living in bodies, and conversing with us, they join with angels, and converse with the spirits of just men made perfect; They are set at liberty from all the sorrows of this lower world; their faculties are enlarged, and they see and know what we desire to, the result of God's dispensations with angels and men.

Death has reached all their virtues and graces into the finishing hand of Eternity, where they are produced before

Him, who is appointed Heir of all things, and Judge of the world, with approbation and applause.—And their bodies that were purchased by Christ, and the temples of the Holy Ghost, shall come forth at the dawn of everlasting day, beautiful and immortal, fashioned like unto Christ's glorious body: Yes, their faithful monuments will render back their dust, and with their bodies, their characters shall rise, and their righteousness go forth. This being the case with our friends who have died in the Lord, why should we stop at the grave to mourn? Rather let us, with Jacob, go on our journey. The first monument ever erected for the dead, was that which Jacob set on the grave of Rachel—"*And Jacob set a pillar on her grave, that is the pillar of Rachel's grave to this day, and Israel journeyed.*" So should we go on to serve God and our generation, and gather fruit to eternal life; then we shall be blessed at our death and our bodies will rest in hope.

But it is time that I speak to those who are this day in mourning, especially to the bereaved companion of him whom we have interred in the silent grave.

MADAM,

Various are the scenes that have passed over you since you were connected with him, who is now no more, by the most tender and sacred ties.—Hand in hand, has he gone with you through the greatest part, by far, it may be, of your days, and has assisted you to bear up under former troubles. When your help and expectations were dashed in a moment, and your soul filled with sorrow, because your beloved son was, in an instant flung out of time into eternity, he bore a part, and relieved your burden in a great measure:—And, before you had forgot him, another promising son, who had almost completed his education, wasted away and gave up the ghost in your embraces.—In these afflictions, your spirit, assisted and supported by your wise and faithful companion, now with his children, sustained your infirmity:—But, now your spirit is troubled,—"*And a wounded spirit who can bear?*"

Your house is left this day desolate and mourns! and you are left alone to draw out the remainder of your days in sorrow—Alone did I say, no; for what is the voice from Heaven?—"*I will be GOD of the widow.*"—To GOD we commend you, in all your trials, may *He* make up your loss in the enjoyment of *Himself*, and prepare you by his grace for that world where the difference of sexes is not known; "*but are all like the angels of GOD in Heaven!*" Hark! does not your spouse speak from yonder loansome place where we have laid him!—Weep not for me, but for yourself and your children!—He is beyond your cares and prayers, and needs not your tears. Turn your attention then to your house, set that in order, for you are soon to follow him, and your sleep will be together in the dust.—Your parting is but short, if you wait a few years longer, the grave will be your house, make your bed therefore in darkness, do what your hands find to do, for in the grave there is no work.

Secure an interest in Him who is the Resurrection and the Life, and be a follower of all those who through faith and patience inherit the promises; then your dying groans will introduce you to the songs of angels.

In the next place, I would speak a few words to the children of the deceased.

My young Friends,

This is to you such a day as you never before saw.—Your tender and indulgent Father, the guide of your youth, whom you honored and loved, is taken from you—you will see his face no more!—No more hear his faithful warnings, his kind admonitions, and his fervent prayers!—You cannot be so unmindful of him, as not frequently to call up to your minds his hollow, dying groans, his wasted remains, and the day of his burial:—When these things occur to your minds, reflect how he would wish to have you live, and consider him, though dead, as yet speaking to you—"*Be ye also ready.*"—Your time in this world is short, your days few and evil, soon they will be numbered and finished, and you will go down to the grave to him. Seek after the God of your father, and serve him with a perfect heart. Make religion the business of your early days, then God will have a favour for you. "*Thus saith the Lord, I remember the kindness of thy youth.*" Let the world be better for you while you are in it, then your death will be precious in the sight of the Lord. Emulate the virtues of your father, and be in special tender and careful of your infirm and bereaved mother; remember she brought you into the world with pain, nursed you and rocked your cradle in hope that you would comfort her:— Now is the time for you to accomplish her desires and expectations:—In your turn, therefore, rock the cradle of her old age, comfort and support her that her soul may bless you before she dies.

He, who before he entered on his sufferings, committed the care of his mother to the beloved disciple, *Saint John*, does this day, in his *providence*, commit the care of your mother, to you, her *only Son*. Be faithful to the trust reposed in you, that you may have peace in your own mind, and before you a glorious prospect. Remember you have a more noble part to act on the theatre of eternity; raise up your views, therefore, to the elevated scenes of immortal existence; and while passing through this world, cultivate an heavenly temper, that your death bed may be comfortable, and your eternity blessed!—Your young and tender years, your animating prospects of enjoying the good things of this world, are no security

against the darts of death, or the attacks of misfortune.—
Use this world therefore as not abusing of it, for the fashion of this world passeth away.

Let other mourners realize the voice of GOD in this dispensation of his holy providence, and prepare to follow their departed friend.—O, that we may all be wise in time, and consider our latter end.

Concerning our friend that has fallen asleep—*we trust in Jesus.*—I am warranted to say, that from his youth, such were his abilities and conduct, that he was justly esteemed by all that knew him.—This appears from the honor conferred on him, the trust reposed in him, and the many departments assigned to him to act in, for the public good. And in every station, he conducted with honor to himself, and advantage to the public. When the oppressive measures of the British ministry rendered it necessary for us, that we might secure the liberties and privileges GOD and Nature had given us, to oppose with force, he stepped forth, took an active part, and with wisdom, prudence and undaunted courage, pressed on through the whole war, 'till the scene of blood was closed, and America declared independent!—And if you would call up former days, when a cloud hung over this land, and your hearts palpitated with fear, for yourselves, your helpless children, your aged parents, and the *ark of GOD;* and see this man animating, encouraging, and leading on to the fight our virtuous sons, that he might secure to us what we now enjoy—you would go to his grave and weep.—"*How is the mighty fallen, and his weapons of war perished!*"—He was a sociable, improving companion, a true and faithful friend; a firm believer in the religion of Jesus, a devout attendant at his table, and one that constantly worshipped God with his house. He was one that studied to make and keep peace in the church, as his fellow disciples know, if they would testify.

This Commonwealth has lost, in him, a wise and faithful Magistrate, and this church a worthy and benevolent Brother: His wife has lost a kind and affectionate husband, and his children a tender and indulgent father.—I visited him on the day of his death, and though unable to say much, whispered, "*That he was satisfied with life, entirely resigned to the will of* GOD, *trusted through His mercy, and the merits of* CHRIST, that he should *have an inheritance among the saints in light—prayed for patience, and that he might* hope to the end,—*and added, that death was not terrible to him.*"

Let us all be followers of him, wherein he followed CHRIST.

I am unwilling to dismiss this crowded assembly, 'till I remind you of the necessity of being actually prepared for death!—On the slender thread of life eternal concerns hang!—If you would have hope in your death, you must have renewing grace in your hearts! You cannot enter into the kingdom of Heaven unless you are born again!— Our sins must be pardoned thro' the blood of CHRIST, and we justified by the grace of GOD, and sanctified and sealed by the Holy Spirit of Promise; or we may not look for a calm evening of life, or an unclouded morning at the opening of Eternal Day! But if we seek after and find the knowledge of GOD and our LORD JESUS CHRIST, at the close of life, when we stand on the threshold of Eternity, we may, with hope and comfort, send up our souls to that GLORIOUS BEING, who gave them,—and our flesh shall rest in hope, 'till the last solemn scene open upon this little ball!—When peals of thunder, such as have not been heard since sin entered into the world, shall play round the Universe;—mountains melt down like wax—and hills and seas return—and the opening Heavens give place for the second coming of the BETHLEHEM BABE, the Calvary Master, the Heir of all Things, the Judge of the World.

Then our bodies shall be called forth, and united to their old companions, and we appear at the Judgment Seat.—May we find Mercy of the LORD at that day!

AMEN.

REVOLUTIONARY JOURNAL OF COL. JEDUTHAN BALDWIN

REVOLUTIONARY JOURNAL OF
COL. JEDUTHAN BALDWIN

DECEMBER 1, 1755   I Workt a clearing out the perade. Caried out the Chips Without the gate & onto the wall begun Around the Perade.

2   Draw the Timber of the perade up onto the Wall & hald. 2 Logs out of the Lake for Bords.

3   the Coll. moved into his house. I was Puld Down with others By a rope, the Well Laid out, Brought into the Camp 187 oxen

4   Being Thanksgiving at NB. I was Comanding officer for to Day & had the Care of killing the Cattle, We Kild a large Number of the Oxen. Laid the Sills of our house

5   I Went to Killing Cattle With all the men. the Drovers Went of. Capt Fay Went of home With many of the Sick.

6   I went to work at my house. Ensign Stone Died and Was Buried. the rest of the Catel are kild

7   I Workt at my house.

8   I Was officer of the Day. the Beasts Cut up and Salted. Capt Whiting Lodged in his house. Several horses Came in for the Sick & Coll. Fay. my Chimny Begun, Mayger Kingsbury Moved into his house yesterday. Pleasant Wether. I Was very Poorly. Went to David Stones Funeral, Who died in the morning.

9   Nothing Remarkable hapend. I Workt at My house Cuting & Salting Beef. I finisht my house. Moved in. Several horses Came in for the Sick from Coneticut. herd of Coll. Bagly at fort Edward.

11   we Cleard the Perade had all the men under arms. Moved S Brown Corpl Metcalf & Thos Layton & Benjn Dolber out of the fort Sick. Went to meet Coll Bagly $2\frac{1}{2}$ Miles Down towards fort Edward

Decr 12   Hald in Col. Plasteds house for a Guard house.

13   thro'd Chips onto the Wall to make room for the Beef. in the forenoon I Was tak Sick. in the afternoon I Had 2 Blisters Drawd & Polticed, in the Evning Exceeding Bad.

15   Being Sabath. I Grew Worse my fever Seteled Which was a Slow fever. I had an Extreem Pain in my head. & Body very much Bound. I continued Loosing my Strength & flesh till the 28 Day by Which time I Was Brought almost to the Gates of the Grave. But God

apeard for me & Bles't the means Used for my Recovery. I had 2 Doctors, Dr. Bliss & gott. I was Well taken care of & my fever Brook ye 28 Day of Decr & then I Begun to Recover Begun to gain Strength but Sloly till the 01 of Janary 1756. by this time I had a good Stomach to my vituals tho Bound in my Body for Wh I took Physic every morning. the 28 of Decr there came in one Desarter.

Janry ye 8 of Janry came in a nother.

10 I eat Some pancakes Wch Lay in my Stomach & hurt me very much.

11 my victuals Did not Digest. Being Sabath it Was Spent in Prepairing to Send letters and much as others have Ben here in time past in Labour.

12 Being the 30 Day Since I Walkt a broad blessed be God for his Great Goodness in Rasing me from a Bed of Sickness to Such a measure of health as that I have bin this Day to Walk out of Doers.

this morning When the Gun fier'd Liet Smith & Eight men went of, after one of the men had Carelessly Shot Sergt Miller in the Leg, a flesh Wound — for Albany With Letters.

13 I went a broad & was very Comfortable. Dr. Bliss came from fort Edward.

14 Capt Engersoll Came from albany, Brot me 2 letters from my father & a nother from my uncle. it Rained hard all Day in Showers.

15 my Brother N. Baldwin was Drooping. it Was very pleasant Weather.

16 it Was Wether Pleasant. Brother N. Baldn took

17 Physick. it sno'd in the after Noon & it was Warm·

☞ James Clerk Died in the after noon Son to John Clerk, he belongs to Pelham, Came into the army from Chester. a post with privet letters wt of in the night.

Decembr ye 1th 1755 Nathaniel Brown from Waltham Was taken Sick took Physick ye 7 of Decr & Died the 18th Day in the morning.

17 Isaac Pratt was not well.

18 Being Lords Day. I Was officer of the Day. there was no Publick work Done all was Still & it Seemed a little Like Sabath it was the most Like Sabath of any I have Seen Since I have ben here.

☞ James Clerk Was Decently Enterd. it's a Spring Like Day. Dr. Bliss Went to Fort Edward.

19 I went the Grand rounds: in the morn. about ½ after 6. o'clock We was all allaramed by Capt Rogerses fiering as he came in on the Lake from ye Lake Champlain Where he took 2 Prisoners & Brought them in with him. it Rain'd in the after noon. I Began to Draw a plan of the fort.

20 It Was a Wet Day a Scout chast by the Indians at South Bay yt Wt from Fort Edward.

21 Cold & Cloudy, Capt. Rogers Lost a man yt Went into F Edward
☞ at Night We had a Dance.
22 a pleasant Day finisht ye Well.
23 finisht the Plan of the fort. I was officer of the Day.
24 fetcht wood over the Lake the wind was South & Warm.
25 Being Lords Day it Was Spent as others with many.

Putnam punisht for Disobeying.
26 Lieut Smith Came from Albany With Letters.
27
28
29 Capt Rogers & 50 men Went a Scout. Joseph Bask Left 2 Dolars and 4 Coppars With me.
30 two of the Scout Returned. at evening Cleard the Parade.
31 two of the Gunners Desarted & was Brought Back about one hour after.
Feb 1 Lieut Woodwell & 16 of the Carpenters Went of for home Caried 2 prisoners to albany.
5 Capt Rogers Scout came in With one Prisoner Left one Sick. 6 waggons came in.
6 I Went to Bring in the Sick. Samll Lion Was Drownded. 5 of my men Wt Down in the Wagons.

Samll Sheppard, Wm. Barrat, Benaiah Studson, Jesse fletcher, Francis Fletcher Wnt home.

7   Nothing Extraordinary Hapined.

8   Being Lord's Day. the Hospittal Was Begun, the Ground Lade oute.

12   I Went a Scout with 21 men onto the top of ye mountains. Sergt Call Brook in the Dungeon.

14   John Doty put under guard.

15   Being Lords Day all Recreation as well as Labour forbiden. Ensign Fales Died & was Buried. John Doughty tryed & Rcd 10 Lashes.

16   I had a letter from S Baldwin. Capt Whiting Wt to fort Edward.

17   25 Wagons came in. Shot at marks. 2 frenchmen Came in from Crn poit.

18   the Wagons Wt of. Liet Brown With ye 2 french Wt to albana.

19   I Wt to Capt Rogerses to Diner.

20   Capt Whiting With Capt Engersoll came up.

21   I Went of With Capt Whiting to fort Edward about Eleven o'clock at Night with 16 men.

22   Being Lords Day, I taryed at fort Edward. People were very modist. Coll Whiting Wt home.

23   att fort Edward in the afternoon I went with 6 Gentlemen to find a Road Down ye River Returned at

night Went to ye Coffe House with all ye Gentn. Revd Mr Norton Came to ye fort.

24 I With 16 men Set of for fort Wm. Henry With Capt Putman & ten men for South Bay & fort Wm Henry & to Carralong. He came up ye Road With me four miles & then turned out East for S. Bay. I got Home at Sunset.

for 3 or 4 Days cold weather.

27 Capt Putman came in.

28 We fixt for a Scout 15 Days.

29 Capt Putnam Joind Capt Rogers, myself & Capt Parker & we marcht With 60 men towards Crown Point N. N. E. 12 miles.

March 1 We Sent back 5 of our men Not well. we marcht North 10 miles. Saw a Wolf Chase a Deer into the water, past Capt Putnams Enterueil Where the indian town of trade, Mass house, cross & Camps all Standing. very fine lands. then aldered N. N. West 4 miles.

2 we Set out about Sun rise marcht over a very Large mountain Cald Parkers mount. traveld N. all Day about 10 miles campt on low land loged not in a fither-bed but on hem lock boughs.

3 we Set out about Sun an hour high traveld N be W. 7 miles. came over Several Large mountains this Day in the after part of the Day we marcht N. N. E. 6 miles a

Snow fell to Day about 4 inches Deep which made it very Slipery & Wett.

4 traveled N. E. 11 miles to Day.

5th We marched N. E. till about 11 o clock & then We came in Sight of Crown point 8 miles then we altered our Cours & marched N. 6 miles. Logd in sight of Crown point without fier. it Snowed in the fore part of the Day But Soon Went of again.

6 about 2 o clock in the morning as we went to Cross the Lake in order to Way lay a Road on the E. Side (for we by Information Expected to find a Small Villiage on the west Side about 10 or 15 miles Down N. from crown point but there is none)—Capt Rogers fell of a Legg of Rocks into the Lake 26 feet With much Difficulty he gott out but it Prevented our Crossing this morning for the Ice was too Weak.

7 Being Lords Day. we had kep very clost all the Day before only as we moved to the Edg of the Lake $\frac{1}{2}$ a mile in order to try to get over this morning. Capt. Rogers With 3 men went to See if the Ice would Bare us over about 3 o'clock in the morning but found the ice too week. we concluded to go and waylay the Road from Crown Point to the Caralong marcht S 12 miles to the Road Where we Lay just be low the Villiage till into nite

8 about 4 o clock in the morning we marcht $1\frac{1}{2}$ mile to the upper Villiage but we hid our Packs on the Point

at a Barn the fields was Plowed which we went thro' & made a large track. I Kept in a house with 21 men Capt Rogers Capt Putnam & Capt Parker Kep in a Barn about N. E. 80 Rods with 34 men Expicting Every minute to take a Prisoner.

Capt Rogers & Capt Parker Wt 3 Scouts this Day but could find none of the french out of Reach of there Canon. we Kept Very clost till after Sunset Without Victuals or Drink. about 9 o clock at Night we Set fier to 9 Barnes & 2 houses (in the Barnes Were Large Quantitys of wheet, Oats and Some pees) & then we came of about S b W 4 miles. in the 2d barn Set on fier was an indian a Sleep which was Burnt So that we had to carry him. Logd on Wett land. Lay cold.

9 Marched about South 18 miles Waded through a River carryed the man Burnt Very much. We followed the Enemy for Several miles. Logd without fier.

10 we concluded to Leave Capt Putnam Capt Rogers & 6 men (& the man that was burnt Nigh the Lake) in order to find a good wagon Road to or by the Caralong and I was to Liad the Scout home & Send Down Battoes in the Lake for them. I traveld S. W. 6 miles crost the Notch of the mountains marcht W. 3 miles came to Putnams Brook marcht S. 6 miles. in the morning we crosst a Road the french & Indian Scout of 160 had made the Day before, Who was allaramed by the Great

fiers at Crown point a Monday Evening, & there Cannon about Day Break a tuesday morning. we lay about half a mile this night from where the french Campt a tuesday night they wrote on the trees that if they could catch us they would Burn us or we Should them Directly.

We Loged this nite without Camp.

11 Marcht S. S. W. 18 miles got to fort Wm Henry about 2 o clock in the after noon the men very Weak & faint haveing Nothing to Eat for Some time.

13 the men under armes Coll Bagleys letters Recd & one of ye Govnt acts.

14 Being Lords Day. Writeing Letters to Send home hardly anything of Religion to be Seen. Capt Rogers came home with Capt Putnam & Smith. about 1 o clock in the morning Capt House Capt Ingersoll & Capt Mason set out for Boston.

15 Capt Rogers Set out for Boston about Sunset Capt Putnam to the other fort.

16 nothing Remarkable hapined. Ensign Taylor Set out to fort Edward with 25 men to bring up Sauce to this fort Wm Henry.

17 The Mohawks Went a Scouting, Set our Potts
18 for fish it being Very Pleasant Weather.
19 all hands Getting Wood. 4 of the Mohawks came Back.

20 Ensign Taylor came in from fort Edward With Sauce for ye Coll.

21 Being Lords Day, Cloudy Weather.

22 We cleared out all the Barracks & the men Shifted.

23 Salting Beaf, Pitching tents.

24 it Snowed. the 4 indians came in from ticonderoga With a french Scelp also inform of 3 large partys coming out from that Place Lately.

25 theire came in 20 odd wagons loaded with Sale chiefly. Salting Beef. Lieut. Wade & Smith, News of Swago being a tact.

26 all hands to Getting Wood. in the fore noon the Wagons went Down all But three With Lieut. Smith, Sarjant Peter Jineson Wt home. about 2 o'clock we was allarmed by the mohoaks fiering that Went Down With the Wagons, Sent 2 men Down to fort Edward to See what the News was.

27 all hands to Salting Beef. a Scout of 43 men from fort Edward at 3 o'clock came here Brought News that the Indians had Scalpt 2 men Belonging to fort Edward about 5 miles Down the River in Moses Crick Who were after fish in a battoe they were Killed in the morning. about 5 o'clock in the afternoon Lieut Smith Returnd with 8 or 10 wagon Loaded with Rum & molasses & Shugar. the Scout from fort Edward went Directly up the lake in battoes in order to way Lay Nigh the mouth

of wood crick. we Sent a Scout Lieut Poor with 10 men Down the west Side at 8 o'clock at night.

28 being Lords Day. all hands to cutting wood the Wagons to bringing it home in the fore noon & Beeting up for volenteers in the afternoon. 2 men this morning from Fort Edward bringing News of 300 of the Enemys waylaying the Road between Fort Edward & Saratogue. a Mohawk came from General Johnson Brings no news. we Sent about noon 4 men in the burch canoe to over take the party that went out yesterday.

29 all hands Getting Cooper Stough. the Scouts came in at night.

30 all hands getting Cooper Stough. Capt Grant & Hobby with there party went to fort Edward.

31 Snoed two men Went to Albana.

April 1 Very cold.

2 Capt Parker Went after cooper Stough With all hands but gott But little.

3 Went after Sader for Whaleboats.

4 Being Lords Day I Servd the Lord with all my Might.

5 all hands to work I hewed Seeder Loggs to be Sawd.

6 Went in the Barge With Lieut Poor & others for Pleasure it was Very Squalley & Bad Sailing.

7 in the morning I went over the Lake after Cooper

Stough Lieut Oggdin came up & Brought the Sorrowfull Niews of the Death of Dr. Samll Brigham of Marlboro.

8 Lieut oggdon Went of for albany I Recd 2 letters yesterday & two this morning two from my father one from my uncle Samll B. & one from John Martyn Jr Jo Bush Died.

9 I went over the Lake after Cooper Stough Set a colpit in the after Noon

10 I Went Down the Lake to Wheelers Island after hooppoles With Lieut Smith, Ensign Sellon, Taylor & Glasier. a Campeign Went with the Berge & 4 Battoes.

11 Sergt { James Archable, James Mc neal, John Mitchell } of Londondary
Isaac Callon of Springfield
Wm. Benit of Framingham
& Jonathan Sillaway
Set out on a Scout Down the Lake

12 Monday morning about 10 minutes after four o clock the Sentrys heard 3 or 4 guns fierd Down the Lake, Soon after a whole realey of 30 or 40 guns to geather, after that Several Scatering guns, we concluded Mc neal was beset & Sent Lieut Poor Down with 9 men in two Batoes to See what the fiering was they went of at 6 o clock and came Back at 2 o clock in the after noon with the Bodies of Mc neal, Callon & Benit, Which they

found Dead on an island about 12 miles Down the Lake. they Were all Stript Shot Scalpt and cut in the most awfull maner we Doubled our guards this night. apost Went Down. Gj h en. We suppose the other three are Either killed or taken as they are not found.

13 Sarjt Akins came in in the morning, in the afternoon we fitted up our guns & about Dusk Sergt Darling with 7 men Went a Scout on the East mountains Down the Lake, he & the men with him See many Enemy & heard more, Several of them followed them up within half a gun shot of the fort we fierd an allaram ¾ after Eigh o'clock at night.

14 Serjt allen came crost from fort Edward with one man more, came away at 12 o'clock at night, & got here about 3 o'clock. we fierd a nother alaram ½ after 4 o'clock this morning. Cleard out all the york armes, filld Sand baggs, Layd 2 platform & made all the prepairation for an attackt that is possible, the Enemy apear very Bold and Dareing.

15 a Long Storm of Rain holds for Several Days in which time they make no apearance the Blew at N. E. which caused the Lake to Run Very high & continued

21 till the 20, all the officers of the Garrison agreed to take there turns to Stand one in Each Bastin 2 hour at a time Every Night all night.

22 Serjt Akin Wt to 'tother fort. Derling Shot all

the french at the uper Iland See the Smoaks on the Side of the mountain.

23 heard Dogg Bark. J. Fletcher Died.

24 Lieut Rogers With 20 men came up, 5 of our Serjts.

25 Lords Day. Sent 2 men Down East to Albany at Night.

26 monday the men Slung their Packs to go home

27 Cetcht a Large Number of Fish Cleard the Garrison

28 Saw Batoes or canoes go off from the uper Island Abel Brown Died & was Buried ye Same Day

29

30 a post from Albany Brings News of Rleiefs coming.

May 1 Raney Day

2 Being Lords Day. indian canoes Seen Down ye Lake

3 Cleared out ye Garrison

4 James Fowler Died in the morning 4 o clock

Decr. 8 1775 Bought Cloth for Great coat.

Decr. 10 1775 Recd. 68 Dollars, Rashon money. paid Hide for Oliver's[1] Coat, Blanket & Sundry articles, & a pair of Long Breaches.

11 finish the Fortification on Cobble Hill.[2]

12   Begun the causey at Leachmor Neck

13   Began the Covered Way onto Leachmor hill. Col. Glover[3] Regt. & Capt. Foster Compy of the Train Marched for Marblehead, upon hearing of 3 men of War lying at that place. bought a Watch for 8£.

14   workt on leachmor point[4] went in the afternoon to Dotchester point to See the mashine to blow up Shiping, but as it was not finished, it was not put into the water.

15   Came from Dotchester & went to Leachmor point to work. Recd a letter from Jesse Cutter. Oliver' Shirts & Geese from Brookfd.

16   Stakt. out the Fort on Leachmor point.

17   went to work on Leachmor point, it was Very Foggy in the fornoon, & when the Fog cleared away we had a Very havey fire from the Ships, & from Boston but thro' Divine goodness we Recd by little damage. Abel Woods was wounded in the Crotch or thigh. workt all night, got our men covered.

18   went down in the afternoon to Leachmor. Wrote to Mr. Forbes.

19   Went upon Leachmor point to work. a No of Shot & Shells were thrown from Bunker Hill & from Boston at us & at Coble Hill, many of the Shot lodgd in our Brest work, & some of the Bumbs Brok high in the are & 2 near our works, but no Mischief done this Day.

20   went upon Leachmor Point we recd a No of 24 lb Shot from Boston into our breastwork & others Just went over all in a direct line hit the wall.   Several Bumbs burst in the air, one was thrown from Bunker Hill into Cambg by Phineys Regt. 13 inch which did not bust went to see Abel Woods found him Comfortable, bought cups & Glass Ware for 7/6.

21   went to Leachmor point in the morning, went to Watertown in the afternoon.   it was Very cold this Day. the enemy did not fire at us this Day.

22   at home Recd Betseys Letter Wrote by Dr. H. bought 6 yds of Garlic 28/ & Sent it to Brookfield.

23   went to Leachmor point in the morning.   Wore Genl. Putnams[5] great coat.   Majr Durkee[6] went Home with Capt. Waterman & Lt Bigham.

24   Lords Day & a very Snowy cold Day.   Cut down the orchard at Leachmor point, & laid the trees round the fort had 4 oxen Drowned coming of ye point.

25   a Very cold Day.   Dind with Genl. Putnam. went upon leachmor Point at Sunset, & then went to Genl Washing. in the Evning.   found & Skind ye 4 drownded oxen.

26   went to Leachmor point.   Laid a platform for the Great Morter workt at the bridge, the Day fair & extreem cold.   Dind with Genl. Washington & Lady.

27 went to Watertown, paid 10 Dollars to pattin. Col. Comings Lodged with me.

28 went to Leachmor point finished the Bridge & 2 platforms in ye loer Baston.

29 Laid one platform for a morter in ye loer Baston & a platform for a cannon in ye upper Baston at Leachmor point. Cold.

30 cut out two embrasures at Leachmor point. a No of guns heard of at Sea, Supposed to be Ships coming in, or privateers Engaged.

31 Lords Day it Rained in the morning. No fateague this Day went to Meeting Mr. Leonard Preacht from Exodus 111 & 10.

Jany 1 1776 the Old Troops went of & left the lines bair in Some parts, cold

2 Took a plan of the Fortification at leachmor point. warm pleasant Day.

3 went with 40 men to work at Leachmor in the forenoon & to Watertown in ye afternoon, a warm pleasant Day.

4 to leachmor point cast the embrasures

5 went to the half moon Batery at Inmans Point, a pleasant Day.

6 to Inmans point & to lechmor point, a Very windy Day.

7 Lords Day, wort the Surceler Battery on Inmans point, & Cut out the obtuce ambrasure in the upper Bas-

tion on Lechmor point, & throwd down the Stone wall there. took a plan of Cobble Hill Fort.

8 finished the Sircular Battery at Inmans Point, & workt with 100 men at Lechmor p. Laid out the west Redoubt in the corner of the orchard at Lechmor point. Major Knowlton[7] with a number of officers & Men crosst the Milldam to Charlstown & Burnt eight Houses & other of the Buildings there which made a great light. left only 6 houses remaining.

9 Begun upon the west redoubt on L. Point it Raind several Showers this Day & cleard off cold just at night when the wind rose & was very high.

10 had 5 teems carting Sodds, laid them in the new works, layd the Abertee round the new works, cased the ambrasure in the uper Redout, & Maised the Epolimey there, this Day Excessive cold and windy.

11 Workt at Lechmor point. Drawd in Abatree Brok ground for the new work, finished laying out the work with Stones. it raind & Snowd in the Evning, & was a cold Day.

12 workt at Lechmor pint had 100 Rifelmen to work with us 200 from Prospect Hill[8] which made 300 in all, but found the Ground very hard frosen a foot thick in general. the oxen workt well this Day raw cold Chilley wind, Col. Miflin gave me a Quire of paper to Draw plans on.

13 Workt at Lechmor point had 4 teems carting

Sods. laid out 2 ambrasures in the west Redoubt. Capt. Dier & Lt. Grey[9] came down & Joined us.

14 Lords Day, workt at Lechmor point Breakfasted, & Supt with Genl Putnam in company with Col Trumball, Mr Hutchison, Majr Cary[10], Mrs Morgan, Capt Abbott[11] & Lady, & Mr Webb.

15 Workt at Lechmor point it was a Raw cold Day and Snowd some. Col Little[12] & Col Serjant[13] were officers of the works. Recd an order from Genl Putnam for wine, the order as follows, viz:

To Commisery Avery Sir
Deliver Col. Baldwin fifteen Gallons of Wine, which is necessary for health & comfort, he being every Day at the works in this Cold Season,
Cambridge Jany 12, 1776.
       Israel Putnam M. G.

a great Whirrawing in Boston, pulling down housen in Charlston & in Boston.

16 workt at Lechmor point. Majr. Megraw officer of the works. a Very Still calm Day a great Stir & Noyse in Boston. we Doubled our Guards in front this night.

17 paid David Kelly 2/6 in full for Shaving & agreed for his Shaving & Dressing hair Every Day for 8/ a

Quarter. workt at Lechmor point Majr Maclary officer of the Fateague a very thick fog till about 2 o clock & then the wind at west cleard of the fog & it raind & Snowd & was a Stormey afternoon & evning.

18 Recd. the News of the Death of Sister Forbes by Dr. Rogers. Wrote to Father Parkman[14] & Mrs. Baldwin. Comisary Avery & Mr. Grey Dind with me. no fateague this Day at Lechmor pint, Recd. the news of the Death of Genl. Magomery & others before Quebeck ye 30 of Decr.

19 went to work at leachmor pint the ground was frosen 22 inches Deep as hard as a rock, & in one night it frose in the trench 8 inches deep so that we pryed up cakes of frosen Earth 9 feet Long & 3 feet broad, it was fair but very cold this Day.

20 workt. all Day at Lechmor point this Day clear & cold, could not dig Sods in the marsh it was so frosen.

21 Lords Day, Stayd at home wrote to Mr. Forbes & Mrs. Baldwin. 13 Ingions came from Canady to see Genl. Washington it was a cold Day went to Col. Gridleys[15] in the Evning. Drank Coffey, & then went to Genl. Heaths[16], spent the remainder of the evning.

22 workt. at Lechmor with a large party. Genl. Washington, Putnam & Gates[17], with several other Gentn came down to see the works. the ground was frosen in 2 feet deep and excessive hard, in some places, the men got

thro the frost, & in other places they did not all, Day rold up an old wall into a line for a brestwork very cold & high tide this Day.

23 workt. at lechmor pint, 13 of the Cocknawager Indians came to see the works, the Regulars in Boston exerrcised on Boston Comon, & went thro many firings. the Day pleasant but a raw cold chilley wind, the ground excessive hard frosen.

24. workt. at Leachmor point, cut Sods had 5 teems carting sods. a Topsel Schooner was brought by the Ice up charls River to new boston with the Tide before she got clear of the Ice. 8 men made there escape from the Admaral' Ship.

25 went to Lechmor point in the fornoon took a draft of Fort No 1 & No 2 in the afternoon. Col. Durkee, Lt. Bingham & other officers came into Camp.

26 Mr. Leonard Came into town. Attended prayers this Morning. the Fateague men all Employed in Poiling up wood & housing Coal &c. I went to Lechmor but no work there.

27 Made a Plan of Lechmor point, this Day Very Cold but fair.

28 Lords Day, went to Meeting Mr. Leonard preached. & in his Sermon Addressed ye close of his Discource to a number of Indians present.

29 went to watertown with Joseph Newell. Sent by him a bag of old Cloaths & a box and firkin. heard that 22 Companies of Regulars wer gone to New York.

30 workt at Lechmor pint.

31 workt at Do. got leave of absents from camp ye Day.

Feby 1 1776 Set out for Brookfield in the Morg. Dind at Wistown[18] Capt. Baldwins, drank Coffey at Northboro, Lodgd at Shrewsbury.[19]

2 Breakfasted at worcester. Dind at Leicester at Mr. Tods with Mr. Allen who accompanied me to my house, found my family well.

3 at home.

4 at home, went to meeting heard Mr. Appelton preach from 1 Peter 3 & 7.

5 went to the South parish to Mrs Welches Capt Uphams[20] & Revd. Mr. Fish.

6 at home.

7 at home.

8 Set out for Cambridge, Lodgd at Shrewsbury.

9 dind at Framingham Col Buckminsters[21] callt at Robert Jenesons & Mr Pigeons, waited upon Genl putnam & Washington.

10 at home in camp. it Stormd Some.

11 Lords Day. workt at Lechmor pint it was a cold Day, the ground frosen very hard 28 inches deep.

we made Very large mines under the frosen Surfice to get Earth to fill the parripets, the outsides of which was partly raised with Stone & part with timber.

12 at lechmor pint. pict. up the Regulars bullets fired towards lechmor on the Ice one man got 80, another 60, & many others got large Numbers. the Genl. officers went upon Dotchester pint.[22]

13 workt. at lechmor. Genl. Washington with a No. of the Genl. Officers came upon the pint. found a good bridg of Ice to Boston.

14 at day Break I arose by the light of 4 fires Shining into my Chamber Windows, Supposed to be housen in Boston set on fire by our people, but about 10 o'clock were informd. that a 2 Detachments of Regulars one from the Castle[23] the other from Boston 10 or 1200 in all, landed at Dotchester point & attempted to take our guard, but were disapinted & they Set fire to 8 or 10 Housen on that pint & retreated to the Castle again. a Snowey Day. I at home. no fateague toDay.

15 workt. at Lechmor. Col Durkee taken Sick, one of our men fell thro' the Ice near Boston, but after 15 minutes he got out himself. bought 50 lemmons 12/ Col Holden officer of ye Fateague.

16 workt. at Lechmor. Mr. Leonard[24] & Dr. Foster came to See the works. the Chanel open up into the bay between Lechmor & Boston

17   workt. at Lechmor.   Genl. Washington, Putnam & Gates came Down to See the works ordered a Guard house to be built. Recd. Mr. Forbes letters.

18   Lords Day. Workt. at Lechmor began the Guard House & diging to Set it in. I went to Meeting in the afternoon.

19   Workt. at Lechmor. afternoon I went to Newton, a prusian came into our Camp.

20   workt. at Lechmor point dug round & undermind large pieces of frosen Earth which we rold out on Skids of Several Tons weight each, in diging for the Guard house, a fine pleasant Day.

21   workt. at Lechmor. 200 men orderd for guard at this place. a fine pleasant Day Wind S. W.

22   workt. at Lechmor. laid up the Timber upon the Polmong befor the guard House a Snowey wet uncomfortable Day.

23   workt. at Lechmor. Raisd. the Guard House 3 prisoners taken at Roxbury. pleasant Day.

24   workt at Lechmor. the Carpenters at work on the guard house a person from Boston confirms the Intelligence that the Regulars were prepairing to imbark. the Vessels were Wooded & waterd. ready for a Voyge with the chief of the heavey Artillery on bord.

25   went to Meeting in the forenoon & to Lechmor in the afternoon began the Chimney.

26 workt. at Lechmor. Discovered the Enemy building a battery on the high ground East from the Magazene at West Boston, where they workt. very Briskly but the air being thick & foggey we could not see clearly at Evning Recd. orders to go to Dotchester in the morning after I had waited on Genl. Washn.

27 went to Roxbury & Dotchester point lodgd. with Col. Learnard in Roxbury.

28 went to Dotchester point. Recd. orders to have Every thing prepaird. to take post at that place. went to Cambridge in ye Evning.

29 went to Dotchester, orderd platforms Laid at Cambridge.

March 1 at Roxbury Laying Platforns for Cannon & 2 for Morters.

2 Building Bumb Batteries, went upon Dotchester Hills[25] with ye Generals recd. there Instructions Dind with them at Genl Thomases.[26] Pulld. down 2 buildings on Roxbury neck in ye Evning. filld. the ambrasures with Abbatree, throd. Shels & Shot into Boston. Split 3 morters this Evning.

3 at Roxbury. a No. of Shot & Shells thrown this Day into Boston. Lieut. Bingham was buried this Day. had everything in readiness for taking post at Dotchester this Night the Congress was split with the 3d Shell or shells thrown from her.

4   prepairing for taking post, an alaram by the regulars by bots going round to New boston went upon Dotchester Hill in ye afternoon the army Came on at dusk with 280 carts & wagons with the materials for the fortifications. 6 works thrown up this night at different places on the Hills & high ground a very Great work for one Night

5   workt. on Dotchester point an alarm about Noon by the Shiping salling down & Regulars embarking on bord. one Man had his hand Shot off.

6   workt. this Day at Dotchester point genl. Washington, Putnam with other Genl. officers was Down to See us. Raisd 2 Barraks.

7   workt. at Dotchester point.

8   workt. at Dotchester point, began a battery on Battery Hill. proposed taking post at Nook Hill.[27]

9   at Do laid out a Battery on the point towards the Castle. Laid out a Work on Nook hill which was proposed to be done this night, but soon after dusk a Very heavy cannonade began at Boston over nook Hill. Killd. 4 Men. among the Slain was Docr Doal of Lancaster & Adams of Brookfd. the Cannonade lasted all night very heavy.

10   at Do, 30 Ships under Sail at once going down, a great Stir in Boston geting Stough on bord the Ships &

by all appearance prepairing to depart, attempted to take post on Nook Hill.

11   at Dotchester, firing all night, opined a battery.

12   atempted to take post on Nook hill, firing all night.

13   at Dotchester point. Recd. orders for to go to New York, went to Watertown Recd. 9. 15. 0 for ye Selectmen for gunns.

14   at Cambridge. Recd. a Warrant for 116¾ of Dollars for Service as Engineer in the Continentall army to the 14th of March Inclusive. went to Roxbury Dind at Genl. Wards,[28] with Revd. Mr. Saml. Baldwin.[29] Recd. a Very friendly Letter from Mr. John Adams Esqr.[30] of the Congress at Philidelphia. Recd. the money above mentioned at Evning. bought a Horse & Saddlebaggs. many things ought to have been noticed from the 4th Day of March to this time which in a hurry have been omited, but peculiar preservation cannot be forgotten by the person Sensible of his preservation.

20	paid at Lt. Scotts[31] of Palmer for Supper, Lodging & horse	0. 2. 5
	Chapin' breakfast & horse hay,	0. 1. 2
	Eli dined horse oats.	0. 1. 0
21	Lodgd. Supt. Breakfast & horse at Hartford Benja.	0. 2. 6
22	willingsford Supper Lod. horse.	

23   Lodgd. fairfield[32] Cables, Dind at Bates.

24   Lodgd. at Capt Knaps, Horseneck.

25   Dind at Kings Bridge. Lodgd. at New York Supt. with Genl. Thomson Genl. my Lord Sterling[33] & a No of other Gentn.

26   Rode in Company with my Lord Sterling & Col. Smith with a No. of other Gentn to view the works round the Sitty & at the west End of Long Island. Dind with Genl. Thomson. Lodgd. at Stocktoms in Broad Street below ye Town Hall.

27   went round to the Several works in Town & out to the Fort at Hellgate or Horns hook where we dind.

28   wrote Mr. John Adams. Laid out some work on Ship battery Hill. at Coll. Smiths wedding. Lodgd with Capt. Badlem

29   Rode round the works with the Genls. in ye forenoon, & in the afternoon gave an order to Capt Bruen for to provide materials for tbe Barrak at fort Ld. Sterling, bought a Cutlass for 16 ½ Dol.

30   began the work' on the old Fort to raise the parapet. it snowd this afternoon Genl. Heath came to Town with Col. Groton' &[34] Several other Regts.

31   Sunday. the men Excused from fateague & the ground was coverd. with snow & water.

April 1   begun the old battery. went round to ye Several works with Genl. Heath & others.

2 went to long Island with Genl. Heath & my Ld. Sterling & others. Laid out & proposed several works there. in the Evning a party of our men, 200, went onto the Island by the Man of war & Set fire to the buildings, brought off Intrenching tools, fowls &c. that belonged to Govr. Trion[35] & returnd Safe. the same night the furnace in this City was set on fire by some Evil minded person, & fled to the Ship, but as it was soon Discovered it did but Little Damage.

3 Drawd plan for 2 Works on Long Island, bought a Coat & Jaceat for 15 Dollars. it raind in the forenoon no fateague the Sitizens Excused from fateague. heard that the fleet was Sailed from Boston. Genl Putnam Came to this City.

4 went Round to the Several works with Genl. Putnam & the other Genl. Officers. in the afternoon I went to horns hook, fort Thomson. a fine Day but windy.

5 to Long Island. Col. Smith went with Genl. Sterling to ye Gersies. I laid out a Battery at ye heighth by ye feray on long Island. I went with Genl. Putnam & Genl. Thomson to Horns Hook.

6 went to Red Hook.

7 Sunday no fateague in the forenoon fireing over the Bay at ye Jersies, our riflemen took 9 & killd 3 of the Enemy, who came to take in Warter, with the loss of only one man wounded. went with Genl. Putnam, Thomson,

Col. Mifflin[36] & Trumbull upon Govenours Island & concluded to fortify that place. 8th. the Ships fell down about 2 miles.

8 went to Red Hook with Genl. Thomson, laid out a Battery on that point, & then I went to Govenours Island, laid out the Fort. at dark one thousand men came on with the tools & went to work & before morning we had a fine trench. it raind all night & was Very uncomfortable. Col. Webb commanded.

9 on the Govs. Isle in ye forenoon, went to ye City afternoon. Genl. Sullivans[37] Brigade came in.

10 went with ye Genl. officers to red hook & to Govs Island.

12 a wet snowey morning. workt on the Fort & Battery with 400 men.

13 wort at the Battery. Genl. Washington came to town, with Genl. Gates & others.

14 workt. at the battery. went to Long Island & to Govenours' Island where the troops workt. Col Prescotts[38] Regt. went over & incamped on govenours Island. in the afternoon I went to Meeting at N. york.

15 the Asia, Man of war went of this afternoon to the great Joy of this place.

went with Genl. Washington, Putnam, & my Lord Sterling to Red hook & to Govner' Island in ye forenoon. Dind with them & spent ye afternoon.

16 to Govenours Island. it raind. Recd. orders to get ready for to go to Quebec.

17 preparing Camp equipage & nessaceries for the Voyge. Col. Putnam came to N. york. Brought letters from Home.

18 preparing for to go to Quebeck. bought sundry articles of Stores.

19 went to the Narrows with Col. Putnam.

20 carried all our things on bord the Ship. Lodgd on Shore in New York.

21 being Lords Day. went on bord Capt. Van burans albana Sloop about 10 o'clock, had a good wind that carried us up the river about 30 miles. lodgd on bord anchord about 8 o'clock.

22 hoisted Sail about 9 in the morning, had a big wind this Day ahead, came to anchor by the highlands ½ after 3 o'clock, could not get thro the narrows. I went on Shore recanortered the Mountains, on the west Side, went upon one about 500 feet high. as the wind continued a head & very high we lay at anchor till about 11 o'clock at night, when the Tide favoured we hoisted Sail & attempted the passage at the highlands, but were obliged to come to anchor before Daylight after passing about 13 miles by Fort Mongomery[39] & Fort Constitution. I was on deck till after 2 o'clock this morning with a Curious eye viewing the Vast mountains & the difficulties in rough

warter. the mountains are said to be more than ½ a mile high almost perpendicular from ye warter.

23 This morning we were at anchor near fort Constitution. after Breakfast Genl Thomson, Col Sinkler, Majr. White, Majr Suell, Capt. Badlam[40], Capt. Van buran & myself with Doctr. & Doctr. & 2 Albana Gent passangers were our Mess in the Cabbin. Capt. Lindley & a Company of Carpenters was on bord our Sloop. we had 5 horses on Bord & 4 Dogs. as the wind was contirary we could not come to Sail. the Genl. proposed my going to view the fort (with him & several others went with us) as I was ordered by Genl. Washington to inspect the whole to the northward where I could do it without retarding our march. and make remarks & send them to him we returnd about 12 o'clock & come to Sail but ye wind continued high & flawey but ye tide favoured, we beat about 3 hours when on a Sudden a flaw took us, Shiverd our Boom all to pieces & carried all before it overboard, knocked down the horses & as I was on Deck it took off my hatt with the rest, which was a great wonder no life Lost or person much hurt. I immediately proposed the making a New Boom, after we came to anchor I went with the carpenters on Shore cut a Tree hewd. Shavd. a drawd. down a boom 51 feet long off from a Mountain a great heighth & got it on board & it was compleatly fixed ready to sail in 3½ hours from the time

the old one gave way, but as the wind & tide was against us we lay at anchor till about 2 o'clock in the morning when the wind abated. some time after my hat went overbord we discover it at a distance. 4 of our men Jumpt into the small boat and brought it me.

24 This is a fine pleasant morning. we were passing the Highlands, as I awoke, in company with several other sloops & then opend a pleasant settld country on each side the river. I went on Shore to several housen on the west side the river, bought butter, bread, milk & eggs, got on bord about 11 o'clock. the sloop kept under Sail had a gentle breeze of wind S. E. we passed by New Windsor[41] & Newboro[42] on ye west Side, Powcapsey[43] & Lime kilns. at Long reach people were throwing wood from a hill 80 feet high to load a Vessel. a Very fine pleasant Day this. about 6 o'clock the Sun went into a dark thick cloud & lookt like a Storm. we passt Livingstons mannor[44] about sunset. kept under Sail till ½ past 1 o'clock A. M. when our vessel ran a ground with 2 other Sloops.

25 yesterday we Sailed about 80 miles. this morning about 7 o'clock our Vessel floated & we had a fine pleasant gale of wind, the weather fair which carried us to Albana 12 miles in a Short Time. we soon marched to our Quarters provided for the Genl. & his Company. Set the Carpenters & Smiths to work making tent polls

&c. we Dind agreably with a No. of our Gentn. of the army & others of the Sity. The Genl. orders that Col. Greatons Regt. March tomorrow for Lake George, Col. Patersons[45] a Saturday & Col. Bonds[46] Sunday, & Col. Poors[47] a monday next, when I am to march with the Genl. Thomson For Quebeck which will compleat a Journey of above 800 Miles since I left Cambridge, but Thank God I have health given to undergo any fateague that I have been calld too in the cause of my Country.

26 Wrote home from albany by Bradshaw, Breakfasted with Commisary Ransler, Dind with Gen. Thomson, Col. Livingstone[48] & a No. of other Gentn at the Kings arms, Mr Varnam. Col. Greatons Regt. marched from albany for Canada.

27 Col. paterson Regt. Marcht. Dind with Mr. Ransler, the armourers came up & joind the artificers at albany.

28 Col. Bonds Regt. Marched of for Canada. I rode with Genl. Thomson, Col. Sincler in a Coach in company with other officers to the Cohoes,[49] crossed the Mohawk River at Lowdons ferry, went to Half mon, crosst Hudsons river & returnd by Stone Robbin to Albany. Drank Tea at Capt Lonsons, had a beautifull Day & a most agreable ride.

29 Supt with Mr. Ray at meriks at albany & Dr. Mchensey.[50] Sent off part of my Bagage with Capt.

Badlem. Dind with Mr Livingstone Commisery Gen., in the afternoon I attended a Treaty between the Indians & Inglish, present a Comtt. of the City & county of Albany, Genl. Thomson & some other officers of the army & about 130 Chiefs & wariers from 2 Tribes of Mohawks, Oniadas, Tuskaroras, onondagos & Kiogos. the Indians were all seated in a large hall, when we went in they arose singly & came round in there turn & Shook hands with all of us, after this serimony was over we were all seated, the chairman of our Comtt arose & welcomd them to this place, was glad to see them in health & peace, & it gave us pleasure to have an opertunity to Smoak a pipe & drink togeather, & then sot down. pipes were brought for every Man with tobaco, then one of the Chiefs arose & said that they were glad to see so many of us there bretheren well & that they had an opertunity to Smoak a pipe with us, then a kind of Quaker meeting lasted near ½ an hour, except some little conversation, Drank some Toddy togeather & then the Genl. Said he supposed that they were Tired with there Long Journey, that they had better sit & refresh themselves with some liqhquer that he Should order, that he Should call them togeather tomorrow, to Smoak a pipe togeather & have some further Conversation as Brothers, & then we withdrew from such a sent (proseeding from the Indians & Tobaco smoak, the room being Crowded), as you can have but a faint Idea of. at night the Indians had a great Dance.

30 put my Bagage a board a battoe. in the morning about 11 o'clock I left Albany with a fair Wind. Dind at Stone robin with Capt. Lonson, went to half Moon, loaded all our Bagage on Wagons, went back to Mr. Lonsons. Lodgd.

May 1 Rode with Mr Lonsin to Saratoga. Lodgd at Mr. Vak.

2 went to fort Miller.[51] Lodgd in a Tent. after visiting Genl. Schuylers Lady & Daughters on the road & Mr Duer at the falls. Lonsin returned.

3 Set out in Batoes & went to Fort Edward.[52] Col. Poors Regt came up. the Carpenters went forward to ye Lake, but for want of Carriages, I stayed with the armourers at Fort Edward Last night. this old Fort is all in ruins, & was set on fire last monday and Continews burning, last night the fire broak out in one of the magazines & burnt most Furiously. Lodgd at Dr. Smith New house on my own bed very Comfortably, in company with Capt. Badlam of the Train of artillery.

4 Genl. Thomson came to fort Edward and went to the Lake. Just at night I set out with 3 load of my Bagage from fort Edward. went about 2 miles & Lodgd at Mrs.

5 went to the Lake with Capt. Newland & Capt. Badlam on foot 12 miles got the Canon on Bord the Sloop with the artillery Stores, the Carpenters & Smiths put their bagage on bord ready to Sail. Genl. Thomson & others came & drank a bottle of wine with me. I supt. with Genl. Schuyler[53] & spent the Evning. Lodgd. in my Tent by the edge of the Lake, a Rough sea that washt down genl Schuylers Chimney as we were Sitting after Supper made us Merry.

6 a Very Rainey Day, prevented the Troops passing the Lake as was proposed. at Evning we caught a plenty of Fish.

7 Set out from fort George, Recd a letter from Genl. Washington informing me that the Congress had advanced my Rank & pay as a Reward of Merit. I wrote a letter of thanks to Genl. Washington.

8 Last night we lodgd at Sabath Day point.[54] Commadore Homes made me a present of 200 Acres of choice land with 2 Housen upon it, which includes the whole of the low lands on & about the point.

in the morning we Set out & went to Ticonderoga Landing. (it rained hard). lodgd in my Tent.

9 got our Bagage over ye carrying place to the fort with the Boats. Dind at ye landing with Genl. Thomson, Col. St Clear.[55] Lodgd. in my Tent by the Edg of Lake Champlain.

10   left Ticonderoga about 11 o'clock. Dind at Crown point, where I took in a No. of Intrenching Tools &c. Lodgd in my Battoe, 8 Miles below Crown point, by the side of the Lake.

11   set off about sunrise Breakfasted at ye Splitrock below the uper Narrows, we passed by the white mountains or Mountain coverd with snow this Day. Dind on an Island 4 Brothers & then set off & Soon was taken with with a high Wind which carried away one Mast & Sale, we made the best of our way for the west Shore, which was about 6 miles, against the wind, we all got safe in after about $3\frac{1}{2}$ hours hard rowing, 4 Battoes & 108 men, but the wind continuing High, we had like to have our boats beat to peices before we could onload & Draw them up. Lodgd on Shore in my Tent. several Indians visited us this Day.

12   the wind continued to blow hard till about 12 o'clock, when it abated, & we loaded our Battoes & rowd of about one o'clock 15 Miles to a Rockey Cove 8 Battoes in Company. Majr. Morgan & Capt. Nelson. we caught a fine Pike fish.

13   Set out about sunrise with a fine wind, went about 20 Miles & the wind faild. we went on Shore got Breakfasted & Set off, rowd to the narrows & then was favourd with a good wind passt by the Island of Noe & on about 6 miles met a Battoe who informd us that the Regular

fleet had arrived at Quebeck, & that our army had retreated about 15 Leagues where they were fortifying.

went to St. Johns[56] where the news of the retreat of our army was confirmd, went over to the East side the river Sorrell. Lodgd at Col. Hasels. we have a Very Gloomey account of our army at Quebeck, the report is that about 500 of our men (chiefly Sick) are taken prisoners with the artillery & stores, but no Sertainty.

14 we wenent down the river Sorell to Shambalee Fort,[57] Where we tarried to get bread baked, (no other provisions to be had hear), In company with Genl. Thomson & the Comtt. from the Continentall Congress, who made me welcom to this place, & advised me to take the Small pox, as that distemper is brief in this place, & I proposed to take the Infection to morrow at Sorell,[58] Docr. Mc Kensey of Pensilvania Regt. to attend me. they are building some armed boats at this place, that will be soon ready for Service. I Just her that all the Intrenching tools are Lost. wrote to Crown point for all the old Intrenching tools to be Sent Down with all the Irons belonging to the old carriages guns. wrote home. Shambalee is beautifully situated on both sides the river, a regular Fort, built with Stone & Lime, without a Trench, well situated by the river, a handsom Church & pritty Villiage, the women are black & no ways inviting.

Shambalee May 14 1776

My Dear

these paper may serve to let you know where I was on perticuler Days, as I have kept a kind of Journal as I have gone a long tho Very Short, it may give you some satisfaction. I have Through Divine goodness, enjoyed my health well & am Very hearty at this time, tho something of a gloom has passed this way, by the retreat of our army from before Quebeck. the report is that about 500 of our army is left Sick with the small pox (& otherwise) near Quebeck which are fallen into the hands of the Regulars with the artillery & what little stores they had there.

15 left Shambalee with a fair wind about 10 o'clock in the morning, Saild Down the River 45 miles, thro a most beautifull Settlement on Each side the River to Sorell, got down about 6 o'clock at evning.

16 Viewd the Grounds on both sides the river with Col. Wait & Col. Antlc.[59] Dind & Drank Tea with Genl. Arnold.[60] Genl. Thomson Came from Montreal. Capt. Barnard, M De la Marquisca,[61] an assistant Engineer came to Sorell. Capt. Badlam movd and took ye Command of the artillery at Sorell.

17 about 10 o'clock this morning I was Inoculated for the Small Pox with Col. Bond, Col. Alden,[62] Majr. Fuller, Majr. Loring,[63] the Revd. Mr Barnham, Docr. Hol-

brook & Lieut Oldham togeather in a mess by Dr. Mc-
Kensey. Genl. Thomas came to this place from Quebeck,
left his army at the three rivers.

18 A General council sot & agreed to move the army
Down to De Shambo[64] as soon as provision arivd, for the
army, which at present is scarce. the Army at ½ allowance.

19 Sunday. this is Observd but all the men at work
that can be employed with tools at three breastworks at
different places, one on the point across the river. order
that all the tool be brought in from the several works to
go down with the army. Col. Greaton Dind with me, &
Col. St Clair Breakfasted with me. laid out some works,
mounted some cannon & got the smiths to work. Genl.
Arnal went last night to montreal.

20 we had the news of Capt. Blisses[65] being taken
(by the regulars & Canadians from Detroit) at the Seeders Above Montreal with the provisions going to that
place. this news gave a damp to the spirits of our people
as hundreds of them had taken the small pox, & others
daily expecting to have it. Genl. Thomas Sick & not
one barrel of provision in the Store & the men at half
allowance for several Days past, & no sertainty of any
coming soon, was truly distressing. I went with Col.
Bond, Col. Alden & Majr Fuller up the river Sorell 13
miles to St. Ours. Lodgd at Col. Duggans.

21 Breakfasted at Col. Duggans, went up 3 miles to Capt. Lamoureux to see our Lodgings & returnd to Col. Duggans. Dind & then went up with our Battoe to our agreable french Landlords Drank Coffey togeather, 60 Barrils of Pork went Down to sorell.

22 Genl. Thomas came up to St. ours sick with the small pox, we heard of our army being cut off at the Siders comand by Majr. Sharburn[66] with 170 men. Majr. Thomas & Col. Dind with us & informd that our army at 3 river wer sent for to com up to Sorell. Col. Dehart went from Sorell with 450 Rifelmen & musketteers to Montreal & the Seeders[67]. the artillery Sent up from Sorell to Shambalee where I was advised to move to prevent my falling into the hands of our Canadian enemy which some fiew now began to show themselves unfriendly. Our Army being very much neglected the supplies not being sent forward in season proper for the support of the army togeather with the distress ocationed by the spreading of the Small pox in the army, & other distempers 2 thirds, were returnd unfit for Duty Ocationed a Cowardly and Shamfull retreat from Quebeck, Deshambo & from the 3 rivers to Sorell & this Day I hear that Col. Poors & Col. Porters Regt. are retireing to St Johns to fortify that place. if this is the case when none persues what may we expect when we are driven by the Enemy.

I walkt about to the Neighbours a Visiting. fair Windy Day.

23 had a restless Night, a hard pain in my head & knees. I got up & after Breakfast I walkt with Col. Alden to Col. Duggans & back again to Dinner, 5 miles, but the pain in my head continewd & several Pox apeard under the skin in my forhead, I eat a little diner, but appetite & relish faild, living 8 Days without tasting the least relish of Salt in my Victuals or tasting any kind of Spirituous liquer.

Just now heard that the Army from the 3 rivers was com up to Sorell. Col. Poor marcht by with his Regt to Shambalee, Col. Porters Regt marched by for St. Johns & they advised me to retire, as it was expected the army would leave Sorel soon, but my french friends assure me that they will take the best care, that I shall have the first notice of any danger & that they will help me off should the enemy persue, at several Housen where I have got aquainted these people are polite, kind & very friendly & are extreemly loth to have us leave them, it gives them great consern to see the army Returning but when Genl. Sullivan Regt comes over the lakes we expect that the army will proseed immediately down to Deshambo, which will secure a Very fine Country & without wich an army cannot be supported there. Just heard that Genl. Arnold had taken a large Store 9 miles above

Montreal worth 10 thousand Pound Sterling, that was going up to supply our Enemies on the great lakes & that he was intrenching & had secured his party & had sent for a reinforcement which was gone to him. this Day I bought a Bushel of the best wheat flowered for 2 pisterenes & am informd that the Inhabitants on the river Sorell rais annually for Sail 150,000 bushels of Wheat besides supplying there families. there buildings are low & mean nearly alike for 45 miles togeather. on both sides of the river it is level without one Hill save a noumber of warter gullies that are short runing into the river, the Barns are thatch roughs & gabel ends & the whole are built without Nails, the buildings stand near as thick as in Worcester Street on both sides all the way on the River.

this Day Docr. McKensey & the Commisary Genl. Visited me, the latter said that he had at the time of the retreat from before Quebeck above two hundred Barrels of Pork & 12,000 weight of Flower in one Store & that the army did not retreat for want of Provision, it was in consiquence of the situation of the army which extended so far that they could not be supported after the fleet & army Should arrive from Hallifax, therefore a Council advised that the army Should retreat to Deshambo, where they were to fortify & make a Stand but 3 frigates ariving with about 700 men Just at the time when our army was prepairing to retire, a general panick seized our army which the enemy saw, they took the advantage, made an appearance, our army fled and left almost every thing valuable behind in the greatist disorder. many of the Officers behavd in such a cowardly manner as brings lasting disgrace on themselves, & others, the Commisary saith that the plunder taken by the regulars left by our army was worth at least 2000£ Sterling besides the artillery & ordinance stores. the Number of our people sick with the Small Pox that have fallen into the hands of the enemy is uncertain yet, but it is said to be small. a great Battle fought but noboddy Killd & noboddy Hurt. by order Capt. Newland, an assistant Engineer, is sent to fortifie St. Johns & Capt Fish[68], an assistant Engineer, is sent to fortifie Shambalee. this Day they left me. a fine pleasant Day.

24 after Breakfast I walkt with my companions round the fields, 3 miles, but felt poor no stomach to diner, head each & full of paine. in the afternoon I rode with my landlord by invitation in his calash to See Genl. Thomson & Col. Campbell at Col. Duggans, returnd very poorly & full of pain & very restless, may God grant his Blessing, if you think this & the other papers are worth preserving pleas to lay them by.

25 I was all this Day so vary full of pain & distress, espetially over my eyes, that I was able to walk but little

abroad, frequently having seveor chills runing thro' my hole boddy which is very tedious to bare.

26 Rested very poorly Last night, & so poor all this day that I was scarce able to look up, the hard fits of Feavour & ague that I had in 1757, nearly resemble this Days Distress, but I walkt a little abroad, as it was a fine Day.

27 rested some last night, and I was much better. this Day the Pox began to come out. Col. Livingston & Majr. Briewer came to see me. a very fine Day. Genl. Thomson Sent me a Horse, Oliver was Inoculated.

28 Slep none last night, a high fevour which made me very restless. I got up early, the feavour abated & I was comfortable, the Pox coming out thick, a soar throat was troubelsom went abroad but little this Day as the air was cold & raw.

29 slept but little last night the pain in my head & soer throat were increased so that I was very poorly in the morning. the weather cold, I was advised not to go to a fire. Genl. Thomson, Col. St. Clear, Col. Maxwell[69] & some other Gentn calld to see me, going to Shamblee

30 Had a very poor Day, my throat very soer a hard head ach & very faint, the Doctr. came to see me & said there is no fear you do well but you have a goodeel to bear yet.

31 Slept some last night felt a little better. a Noumber of Battoes went up from Sorell to Shambalee with Provisions. a good Day. a report spread that 1000 regulars & 5 thousan canadians were at 3 rivers coming up on us. many of the french Inhabitants movd there families to Shamblee & St Johns, we perswaded others not to leave there homes yet, it would be time enough to go with us.

June 1. Slept better last night, my throat better but Stomach Very Soar & Squamish loathing every kind of food. the Pox this Day began to fill, the Nurse counted 40 on and about my face. a rainey Day. Genl. Thomas Died of the Smallpox.

2 rested better Last night, the Pox turnd this Day, my stomach Very fowl, breath bad & my whole fraim Soar. this Day Docr. Stewart came to See me, who informd that Col. St. Clear was going from Sorell with 700 men to 3 rivers. a Schooner & 15 battoes passt up this river from Sorell to Shambalee with provisions & Stores. heard Genl. Thomas was Dangerous.

3 Genl. Woohoe went to Sorell. a Schooner went by from Sorell to Shambalee. I remaind exreemly Soar espetially in my feet. heard of the Death of Genl. Thomas at Shambalee.

4 part of Genl. Sullivans Briggade passt to Sorell in 56 battoes. Capt. Badlam calld to see me as he was

goind to Shambalee. I took Physick to carry off the pox. a pleasant afternoon.

5 Last night & this Day I broak out all over as thick as possible which caused a surver itching. we Just heard that Col. St Clear was returning with his party as he saw Six Ships of war at ye 3 rivers & 30 transports with a land army of 4000, also Just heard that Genl. Worcester was gone home. I think our affairs Look Dark, matters dont go on right, & I dont know how they Should when the Genl. of the army, Schuyler, the Commisary Genl. & Quartermaster Genl. are all in a nother Country, but good conduct & 1 or 2 Victorys in battle may turn the face of things. Doctr. Stewart came from Sorell to see me, Lodgd & is to return in the morning to sorell. Col. Porter Went to sorell. a pleasant Day.

6 I had a high fevour last night, my Boddy being all coverd over with the pox, & an extreem fire and itching made me Very uncomfortable. Col. Starks Regt. went to Sorell. this Day Mr. Grant a Cannadien Mert informd. that a large Fleet was arrivd at Quebeck with 13,000 Regular Troops, a part of which were near Sorell. Genl. Thomson wend down the River with 1500 men from Sorell to 3 Rivers, where we heard the Regulars were landing.

7 Rested poorly Last Night. the burning & Itching of the pox was very Tedious to bair. This Day I took

Physick that workt severely, but I was comfortable before night. a pleasant Day.

8   this morning we were awaked at day light with the report of Cannon Down the River which continewed with Short Intermissions till about 9 o'clock. the cannonade was Very heavey supposed to be Genl. Thomson ingaged with the Regulars. God give us the victory.

9   I rested very well last night, this Day the Pox that came out very fine the 5th, began to turn, & I was better at my Stomach. Col. Pattesson, Majr. Scott & 4 other officers dind with me. Just at evning an Acct was brought that Genl. Thomson had engaged the Regulars at ye 3 Rivers,[70] & got the advantage drov of the main body & had taken about 400 prisoners & was returning with them, his amunition being nearly Expended, and was again attacked by 900 Regulars, who got the better of our troops, killing & taking number, & when the informer came away, the Regulars was persueing & our troops fleeing before them.

10   Col. Dehaws[71] & Capt. Nelson & Capt. Butler[72] calld to see me as they were going to Sorell from the Seeders with there army. they complaind greatly of Genl. Arnolds conduct at the Seeders that it was all togeather owing to him that the regular army with the canadians were not cut off & our prisoners retaken. Majr. Sull cam up to St. Ours[73] Sick with the mumps.

Capt. Scott came up from Sorell as informd that Genl. Thomson' army was returnd to Barkee that they had left about 20 men killd, which was inconsiderable compaird with the loss of the Enemy, which is said to be above one hundred. Genl. Sullivan Sent out orders for 2000 Cannadian militia to go down armd to Sorell to the assistance of our army.

11 I set out from the parish St. Ours for Shambalee in a battoe. I am Very weak & coverd with the scales of the Pox & unfit to travil. Col. Bond & Col. Alden go with me. Our Servants out full with the small pox but not bad. Oliver has it Very light. we Dind at Armarble Ourashe on the west side the River, where we had a fine diner & was kindly Entertained then we went up the River to an old & good farmers where we lodgd & was kindly entertaind.

12 went up the River about 6 miles to Mr Ledjuay' where we were Very politely Entertained where we lodgd. a fine Day but wind a head.

13 went up the River after Breakfast to Point Oliviers where we Dind at a Mass House with a french Preist & was very agreably Entertaind by the Fryer, Mr. Lotbiniere. after Diner we went to Shambalee. Col. Hazel & Col. Antle informd me that there was at this place & St. Johns and about them 2900 men Sick, chiefly of the Small pox that belonged to our army, which has broak

us so that we are poorly able to defent against so superior a force as we hear is coming against us & that Very nigh.

14. Last Night I lodgd in my Tent without taking any cold, & am very comfortable. I Breakfasted with Genl. Arnold, who Recd a letter while at breakfast from Genl. Sullivan informing that he had recd a letter from Genl. Thomson who was a prisoner with the Regulars, with Col. Erving[74] & Docr McKensey. Col. St. Clear was Just come in to Sorell Just alive thro fatiugue there is about 100 of our men Still missing, but they hourly come scattering in, it is uncertain how many we have lost in this desperate action, it is reported that the 2 frenchmen Genl. Thomsons guides were Trators, there is but little dependanc to be put upon any of them. we Just now hear that 10,000 of our enemies are landed on an Island oposit to Sorell about one mile distant. our camp is poorly fortified, & our forces not a third in number that the Enemy is said to be, Genl. Burgoin[75] the most Experienced Gen. in the English service Commands them. I am going tomorrow to St. Johns to give directions to fortify there in order to Cover our Retreat, which I think must be soon without a miricle is rought in our favour, I hope we Shall be able to retreat with all our Artillery & Stores to Crown point, which is the best that I can reasonably expect of hope for, there to make a Stand let what will come

15 we were all Employed in getting Battoes, Artillery & Stores up the Rapids & to St. Johns, the army from Sorell came up to Chamblee. I went to St. Johns Laid out and directed some works at St. Johns & rode back to Chamblee. Kept the men at work geting up Battoes, it Raind all night Very hard, Supt. & lodgd with Genl. Sullivan, Col. St. Clair, Col. Vorce[76] at Col. Hazens[77] in the fort Chamblee.

16 Sunday. Cleard the fort of all the Stores at Chamblee got the Baggage away. I was orderd to the head of the rapids to forward the Intrenching tools & then to St. trace[78] half way between Chambalee & St. Johns, where I had the most Savere fateague in Loading the Battoes with the Stores & Baggage brought from Chambalee in carts to this place to get them above the Rapids, the Vast No of Men sick & in the most distressing condition with the Small pox is not to be discribed & many officers Runing off Leaving there men by the Side of the river to be taken care of by me or others. about 1 o'clock it was reported that the Regulars were at Chambalee & were coming forward but it provd a mistake but it had the effect of sending great Numbers of officers & Soldiers upon the run to St. Johns, & Some to the Oile of Noix[79] & others could not be Stopt till they got to Crown point.

17   I lift St. Trace ½ after Seven O clock at Evning in the last Battoe & Got up to St. Johns about 11 o'clock at Night extreemly fateagued. Lodgd with Genl. De Woolke.

18   this Morning the Genl. calld a Genl Council, which advised to abandon St. Johns, dismantle the fort and carry off all the Stores of every kind. we immediately Sent off all the Battoes to the Oil of Noix with the Sick & with Stores, & the Battoes returned before night for more & by 6 o'clock Every article was in the Battoes, the most of which went of & then we set fire to all the buildings on both sides of the river burnt & Distroyed St. Johns & then I came off in the last Battoe with Genl. Arnold, & got up to the Oil of Noix about 12 at Night but had neither Bed or blanket & lay upon the thawt of the Battoe till day light, it was cold.

19   this Day a number of Battoes came up that were heavey Loaded to this place bring every kind of thing from St. Johns, which thus far is the most Speedy & good Retreet from a Country that it was not possible for us to command against so great a Superiority of force, Just in our rear. the Sick were orderd of to crown point, with the Doctors & the Carpenters & Smith to go also in the morning.

20   this morning I recd orders from Genl. Sullivan to be ready with my bagage & Intrenching tools on bord my

battoe to go with him up the Lake to look out a Convenient place to fortify or to proceed to Crown Point. about 4 o'clock I left the Oil Oix Noix with orders to go to Crown point with Col. Aldin, Capt. Ayres & Mr. Winslow the paymaster Genl. with his Millitiary Chests & I with the Intrenching Tools. Lodgd on the East Side the Lake below Iron pint. missquetoes very Thick

21 Breakfasted at Iron point[80] or point O Fray with Rd. Mr. Barnham. Lodgd on an Island below Cumberland Bay. Dind at the Isle of Mot.

22 crosst Cumberland bay in the morning the surf high. Lodgd on the west side the Lake where we were Extreemly tormented with flees.

23 Came out a little way as the wind was ahead. Breakfasted at the Split rock. Lodgd on ye West Side the Lake below Crown point 10 miles

24 Came to Crown point about 12 o'clock.

25 onloading Battoes & Sending them to Aux Nox

26 & 27 Securing the Stoers & taking Care of the Sick, & Sending Battoes down to the army.

28 this Evning about 5 o'clock the camp was Allarmd by 6 Indians at about 2 Mile distance across the bay who came to the saw mill & carried of one man, but did no other damage. a man died at this place this Day.

29 Put the Powder in the Ice House which was fitted up for a Magazine I rais a House for myself to live in.

30 Heard by Mr Torey, that Genl. Gates was coming to take the Command of this northan army. the Carpenters geting timber to repair the Stone Barraks in the Fort, the Fateague Men with the train continued geting the Cannon out of the Battoes, with the other Stores. I Drank Tea with the paymaster & Mrs Tucker, finished a great Oven.

July 1 part of the army came up the Lake.

2 Genl. Sullivan Returnd to Crown point with the Army & Vessels.

3 proposed to Cover the army by Redoubts, one of which was begun, but the men chiefly imployed in securing Stores.

4 a Genl. Court Martial Set for the trial of a No. of Officers & Soldiers.

5 Laid out Som works on Chimny point,[81] Genl. Schuyler, Genl. Gates & Genl. Arnol came to this place in the evning. 200 Men went to Cumberland head.

6 a Council of the Genl. Officers was held this Day. I dind with the Genls.

7 Recd. orders to go to Ticondaroga with Som Carpenters & to cary all my Baggage, I collected all the Intrenching tools togeather.

8 went to Ticonderoga, with Genl. Schuyler & Genl. Gates, Viewd the grounds on the East Side ye Lake with Col. Trumball on one Hill, took 26 Carpenters with me

to repair ye Vessels & the Saw mill at Skeensboro.[82]

9 Viewd the Grounds on the east with Genl. Schuyler & Genl. Gates, round the peninsula, found Water by diging on the top of the Hill. Genl. Sullivan came in here.

10 Went over & Marked out a road from the North point to the top of the Hill with Col. Wain[83] & Col. Trumball. Genl. Sullivan Reconoiterd the Hill with me. I went up East Creek to the Head about 6 miles, a muddy bottom.

11 Went over to the point with 200 Men to Clear a road, Dig well, &c. it was a Very rainey Day. we returnd about 12 o'clock to camp, Very wet.

12 at work on the East Side.

13 at work on the East Side. Genl. Waterbury[84] came in. I Supt. with the Genl. & other officers.

14 on the East point as Usual.

15 on the East point begun a 3d Vesell.

16 in the morning between day and sunrise I heard some persons say that how come that Chest open, another person answerd sombody has robd it they have pulld up the tent pins & taken the chest out, upon which I arose in my shirt & went out & found 2 friendly Officers lamenting my loss, I examind & found that I was robd of my Hatt, a Camblet Cloak a Surtoot, a blieu Coat & Jacoat full trimd with a narrow Gold lace, a pair of Silk

breeches, a Snuff colourd Coat turnd up with white, a Velvet Jacoat, 3 Cotton & 3 Wollon Shirts, 3 Stocks, 2 linen Handkfs, 2 pair of linen & 2 pair of woolen Stockings, a pair of Silver Shoe & knee buckels, a Surveyors Compass or theodiler, & between 35 & 40 Dollars in paper money, an ink pot, a knife, key & a Number of papers, & other articles. I immediately sent to all the Commanding officers present, & at the landing, acquainting them with my loss, the Army was all turnd out & a genl. Sirch made but none of my things found. I borrowed of a friend, a Coat & Jacoat & hatt, for I had none lift, I was Stript to my Shirt, my breeches & watch that lay under my head were saved only. Just at evning I heard that my coat turnd up with white & Velvet Jacoat was found with the buckles &c. in the pockets, hid in a blind place.

17 in the Morning a part of my Compass was found broak to pieces & soon after the rest of it except the Needle. this Day I wrote to Genl. Sullivan to remind him of the request I had made of a discharge from the Army, desiring him to use his intrest in my behalf while at the Congress, as I am heartily tired of this Retreating, Raged Starved, lousey, thevish, Pockey Army in this unhealthy Country.

18. Visited all my workmen as Usual but found many of them Sick & great complaints of the want of provision,

yt they had only 12 ouz. of pork & 1½ lb of Flower pr Day

19 a Very Heavey Rain last night & continewd the chief of the Day. 2 men of Col. De Haas Regt. were found in there tents drownded in warter, many others lay half coverd or Set up all night. such a heavey Rain is sildom known. this Day by Genl. Gates order I Recd 98 Dollars which will enable me to purchase Cloathing, if I can find them, but they are very scarce & deer.

20 over at the point. it raind.

21 over at the point. a very Showerry Day

22 I wrote to Congress.

23 Laid out the park for the artillery on Rattlesnake Hill, bought Carpenters tools of Six men & then discharged them.

24 Dind with Genl. Gates, & in the afternoon we went round the old French lines with Col. De Haws, which our people were at work Very fast.

25 Genl. Gates & several other Officers went over to the point with me & highly approvd of the works that I had laid out there, & ordered that 220 men Should work daily at least & as many more as could be imployed & was in high good humor. Genl. Gates this Day treated me with high respect and inqured if I had sent the letter, (that I had shown him 3 Days before requesting a discharge from the Army or rather a resignation), and that

I must not think of it, I told him that the Letter was not gone but that Col. Antill had got it, who was going to Philadelphia he said that he would write to the Congress to do somthing more for me & that I must not think of leaving the service, so that it is uncertain whether I see home so soon as I a fiew Days ago thought of.

26 Recd a letter from Col. Smith of New York. Recd a nother Letter from Capt. Hayes giving a perticular acount of the Publick affairs there, the Letter from Col. Smith is Very polite & complisant but a nother letter I recd this Day from my Lucy worth all that I have seen since I left New York, as it is the first that I have recd from her since I left Albany or even of having the pleasure of hearing from home. This Day there is a supply of fresh provision, & it is ordered that all the troops shall have 4 Days fresh & 3 Days Salt meat a week.

27 went over to the East point with Genl. Arnold & Col. Trumball. we orderd the encampment of the Briggade to be alterd. Recd. 200 Dollars to pay for Tools, by order of the Genl. Esqr Gillliand dind with me.

28 this morning I visited all the Artifficers before breakfast as Usual. I paid Esqr. Gilliland 212 Dollars for Carpenters tools as there is no Quartermaster Genl. at present with this army, I have that duty to do in part, & I have the intire direction of all the House & Ship Carpenters, the Smiths, Armourers, Roap makers, the

Wheel & Carriage makers, Miners Turners, Coalyers, Sawyers & Shingle makers, which are all togeather 286, besides the direction of all the fateagueing parties, so that I have my hands & mind constantly employed night & Day except when I am a Sleep & then sometimes I dream.

29 went over to point Independancy with the working parties, this Day a French Malitia officer came into this place from St. Fransway in 20 Days, he informs that all the Indians Refuse to act against us. this Day I dind with Genl. Gates in Company with Genl. Arnold, Col. St. Clair, Col. Dehaws, Col. Wain, Col. Johnston[85], Col. Antle, Col. Ogden[86] & a No. of other Officers on fine Boild & Roast Beef &c.

30 at Ticonderoga & lodg in the Redoubt East of the Garrison in the point of Rocks, but as my business calls I am on Mount Independancy[87] some Days 2 or 3 times in the Day as was the case this Day. Majr. Hay was Appointed D. Assistant Q. M. & began his service.

31 This Day I was over at point Independance and at the French lines, on the Heighths.

August 1 This Day All the Regts. turned out to work at the new battery which was Visited by the Genls. & a No. of Other Gentn, who all highly approved of the work. at Sunset one howet was fired on board a large Gundalow by way of experiment, the Shell brok in the air, one 13 inch Bomb was also thrown from the same Gundelow on bord of which were about 20 men, when the Bomb went of the Morter Split & the upper part went above 20 feet high in the Air over the mens heads into the water & hurt no man. the peice that blowd of weighd near a ton, I was nigh & saw the men fall when the morter burst, & it was a great wonder no man was kild.

2 this morning I went early to Independant Point where we Charged the other 13 inch morter, by way of tryal, when she was fired she burst Just in the same mannar (only this was on the land, & the other was upon the warter) that the other did near about the middle the whole length, so that we have no large Morter here now, these 2 morters were carried from this place to Cambridge & brought back & went Down to Canada & then back to this place, at an immence cost, altho they were worth nothing. Recd by Genl. Gates's Order 300 Dollars to pay for Tools, & other articles wanted in the army. in the afternoon I went round to see how the works were carried on at the french lines, found the works going on fast.

3 laid out the ground for the Laboratory & Store near the park on Mount independance, drawing timber togeather for those buildings, wrote home by ye post.

4 this Day 2 french Inhabitants came in from St.

Johns, who inform that a french fleet had arived in Canad River, & that the Regulars were all but about 200 were gone from St. Johns & Chambolee to Quebeck with there artillery, but they know nothing of Capt. Biglow[88] that went with the Flagg, or of Capt. Willson[89] who are not returnd. 600 of the malitia arivd on the other side ye Lake, 2 miles from the Fort & several came in for provision &c.

5 in clearing the guns on bord of one of the gundelows one of the cannon went of as they were charging it & Killd the gunners mate he was blown into many peices & scatterd on the water. this afternoon I found in an old theifs pack, who was discharged & going home my Sartoot, silk breeches & 2 pair of Stockings, the thif is now confind in Irons in the dungeon.

6 this Day Lieut. Whitcomb returnd. from a Scout, has been near St. Johns, but brings no acct. of our Flag, or of Capt. Willsons party, & and that there is to appearance near 2000 Regulars at St. Johns. this morning I found my Hatt with a Serjant, in the afternoon a lad discoverd a pack in a Chimney which containd my Cloak, Laiced Coat & Jacoat, so that I have found my Cloathing, except my Shirts, 3 pair of Stockings & som Necks. the Needle to my Compass, & Cash I have not found.

7 this Day Majr. Stewart,[90] Col. Courtland,[91] Col. Hartly[92] & Capt. Bush[93] Breakfasted with me. Majr.

Hay & Lady Came to Bord & Mess with me. this morning 2 of my shirts were found and some evidence apeard with the finding of the Hatt & shirts, against Serjant Majr. O'briant who desarted yesterday, & Genl. Gates this Day sent an officer down to fort Edward or albany to apprehend & bring back the desarter of whome I hope to get the money & all those Stolen goods I have lost. I let Lt. have 12 Dollars to bair his expense in his Journey after the thief.

8 2 of my Cotton Shirts were found & a fair prospect of finding the rest. I laid out a redoubt on the North end of the french lines by the lake. Breakfasted with Col. St. Clear, mad up a pay roll for the artifficers.

9 Dind with Col. D. Haws with large No. of Gentn. in the Brush Hall. in the afternoon I went over to the East point with Col. Hazen, Col. Antle, Col. Graton, Mr. Yancy & others. this Day we hear that a reinforcement was com to Genl. How at York, 4000 of them, Provincials troops coming in to Skeenboro & to this place.

10 this Day the paymaster Genl. dind with me & the Commisery Genl. with several other Gent. Made up the pay roll for the artifficers of all Trades.

11 went over to Independant point with Genl. Gates & Arnold to view the works. they exprest entire satisfaction. in the afterNoon I Recd. (by a warrant from the genl.) 1262 Dollars to pay the artifficers under my care.

12   Last night about 12 o'clock Capt. Biglow returnd with the flag from the regulars after being detaind about a fortnight at the Oil Oix Noix, where he was treated with coolness, & sivility by the Regulars.   when he went to that place there was not more than 50 Regulars, the day after he arived there a reinforcement was Sent up from St. Johns.   Capt. Stevens & his party about 35 men were all taken by about 80 cannadians & Regulars in burch Canoes Surrounded him & obliged him to surrender.   Lt. Whitcom[94] when he was on his scout between St. Johns & Chamblee discoverd an officer on horse back coming towards him.   he secreted himself till the Officer came up & then he fired at & wounded him, but his horse carried him off.   we hear by Majr. Biglow that the officer was Brigadear Genl. Gordon of the Regulars, who died of his wound the next Day.   Majr. Biglow carried 2 small chests of clothing for 2 of our officers who were prisoners with the Regulars in Canada, but they would not receive them.   they are brot back.   Just as Majr. Biglow was coming of an officer deliverd him a letter to George Washing Esqr. which he very cooly recd. with Genl. Carltons[95] Orders which are very Insolent as followeth, viz.   Chamblee, August 7th. 1776.   Parole St. Jerome   Counter S. Paris   Genl. Orders   His Exelency Genl. Carlton Orders the commanding Officers of corps will take spetial care every one under their Command be

informd yt messages or letters from Rebels or trators in arms against their King, Rioters, disturbers of the publick peace, plunderers, Robbers, assassines, or Murderers, are on no account to be admitted; that should Emisaries from such lawless Men again presume to approach, whether under the name of Flag of truce men or ambassadors, (except when they come to implore the Kings mercy) their Persons Shall be immediately seeised and committed to a place of confinment in order to be proceeded against as the law directs. there papers & letters for whomsoever, even for the Commander in Chief, are to be delivered to the Provost Martial, that unopened & unread they may be burnt by the hands of the common Hangman, at the same time the commander in chief supposes that neither the assassination of Brigadear Genl. Gordon nor the late notorious streach of faith resolving not to return the troops and Canadian taken at St. Johns in exchange for those rebels who fell into the hands of the Savages at the Seeders & Quenchen purchased from them at a great price, and restored to there Country on those express conditions, be not imputed to the provinces at large, but to a fiew wicked & designing Men who first deceivd themselves, by these misled, the credulous multitude, to the brink of Ruin. afterwards usurped authority over them established a dispotick Tyrony not to be born, & wantonly & foolishly endeavor to provoke the spilling the Blood of our unhapy Countrymen of this Continent in hopes of covering over there own guilt or confirming there Tyrany by the general disturbance of there Country. let there crimes pursue those faithless bloody minded Men who assart that Black is White, & White is Black. it belongs to Brittons to distinguish themselves not less by their humanity than by there Valyor, it belongs to the Kings Troops to leave the blood of his deluded subjects whose greatest fault perhaps is having been deceived by such men to there own distruction, it belongs to the Crown, it is the duty of all faithful servants to restore from oppression and restore to liberty the once free and happy loyal people of this continent, all prisoners from the rebellious provinces who desire to return home, are to hold themselves in readiness to imbark at a Short notice, the Commisary Mr. Murry shall visit the Transports destind for them and see that wholsom provisions necessary cloathing with all possible conveniency for theire passage be prepared for those unfortunate men. they are to look on there respective Provinces as there Prison & there remain till further enlarged or summoned to appear before the Commander in Chiefs of this province, or any other commander in Chief for his Majesty, for the Time being, which Summons they Shall Obey. Genl. How will regulate there place of Landing.

13   Genl. Bricket[96] came in from No. 4 with others.

14   laid out a redoubt on Independant Mount, which Genl. Gates & others aprovd. of.   Dind with Col. D. Hart & Wain.

15   Raised the Labratory. Laid out & began 2 Ridoubts on the North end of the old french lines in the afternoon.

16   laid out a Redoubt on the North side of the point with Col. St. Clear & Cap. Newland, went over to Independent Point Col. Hasel, Col. Antle, Col. St. Clear, Col. wain, Col. Maxwell, Col. Trumball, Majr. Stewart & others had a fine Dinner, they dind with Majr. Hay & myself.

17   Laid out a wharf at the South side of Independant point & orderd a large Stoer House to be built & also 2 guard housen & then I returnd with Col. Wain & Col. Trumball, went into the woods near the Saw mill by a Spring where we had a fine dinner, Venison roasted on Sticks Indian fashon, an Elegant Entertainment made by Col. D Haws, Col. St. Clear & Col. Wain at which the Genl. & about 15 other officers were present. a fine afternoon.

18   I went to Independant point, I returnd with an invitation & dind with the Genl. in Compy with about 20 other officers.   Comadore Winecoop confind by Genl. Arnold.

19 Dind at home Majr. Hay & his most agreable Companion with Lt. Lukes dind my family out at Mr. Adameses where I was invited but the hurry of Business would not admit of going.

20 went with Genl. Bricket to the Redoubts laid out a 1/2 Sircler one

21 over at the point to the workman.

22 Dind with Capt. Ayres. went over to Mackintoshes, ordered the Setting of the Great Store house & Supt. with mrs Hay, Mr. Raiment went away.

23 Dind & Supt with Genl. Gates & Recd a letter from Esqr. Gilliland.

24 laid out a Redoubt on the N. W. side on the plain at the old French lines.

25 went out to the Sawmill to loo out a Suitable place for 2 Regts to incamp Genl. St. Clair, Col. Wain, Col. Allen & Capt. Dow went with me, Genl. Gates, Genl. St. Clair, Col. D. Haws, Trumball, Lewis, Majr. Steward & Docter Cannada dind with me in the afternoon. Recd. a letter from Genl. Thomson informing that he was at Quebeck harbour, Ready to Sail the 5th of August with all the prisoners in Canada going to New York, this letter came by two prisoners who had liberty to return to there homes on the Lake by them we larn that the Regulars are in a readiness to pay us a Visit

26   a very Rainey Day I wrote & was paying of my workmen all Day.

27   a very Rainey Day.

28   it raind hard & was dirty weather. Dind with Genl. Gates & Supt.

29   Genl. Bricket & Capt. Newland Dind with me. Concluded to build a Saw mill. began to hiew the Timber in the afternoon Mr. Lucas went of for Philedelphia we double mand our Smiths fires & workt in all the Shops both night & Day to get the Shiping riggd. & the artillery mounted.

30   Took Physic, was poorly, but went out a little upon business ordered 20 Men to assist the Carpenters geting timber to 1/ pr Day the time they are about the Saw Mill.

31   the Lee Gundalo & Row Galley Saild from this Down the Lake Sent a party down the lake to bring up the Runing Geers of Mr. Raymonts Mill, Col. Brewers Regt. & Col. Phinneys[97] Regt came in this Day. yesterday Departed this life my very good friend Coll. Bond & this D was buried under Arms after a suitable discourse, & Prayer. a discharge of Cannon at the Fort much lamented by his brother officers. he lay Sick about a Week & died with the yallow feaver.

Sept. 1   went out early in the morning with Genl. Bricket to lay out som works, but it raind & previnted it. I made up a pay roll for 3 companies of Artifficers. Col. Waile, Majr. Schult & Capt. Crague[98] dind with me & in the afternoon I went to Mr. Hitchcocks[99] Meeting.

2 went over the water to the point & then to the Mills to lay out Col. Brewers Encampment. Col. Brewer & Docr. Honeywood dind with me.

3 Gen. St. Clear, Col. D Haws, Col. Lewis[100] dind with me. I supt with Genl. Gates.

4 Breakfasted & dind with Genl. Gates.

5 went round the works & over to the point & in the afternoon to the Mills to order the Encampment of Col. Willards Rigiment. this Day Recd a letter from Genl. Schuyler, wrote at albana informing of a Battle at New York, that the enemy had lost 6 thousand, & that we had lost 3 thousand, that Genl. Sullivan & Genl. Sterling were missing, but nothing to be depended upon, as the report was Verbal to Albana.

6 this day I dind with Majr. Sherburn at Independant point. we again hear that 1200 Regulars & 600 provencials were killd. in the battle on Long Island & by a letter from Col. Hartly at Crown point we are informd that a Very heavey Cannonade was heard down the Lake for about 3 Hours, which I suppose there must be an Engagement between our fleet & the Enemy.

7 all hands at work at Daylight prepairing our batteries against the worst.

8   I was Very poorly this Morning as I had been yesterday & last Night I Took Camphire that made me Swet all night, this morning took a portion Rubarb that workt very kindly. in the afternoon I went out to Col. Brewers & Willards Encampments & laid out a fort on the Top of the Mount, North of the Mills. no news from our fleet. this Day a party of Canadians & Indians were discoverd between this & crown Point.

9   I was Very porly with Hard pain in my head & Eyes. at Evning took a Vomit that workt well but kept me up part of the night. heard that the Regulars lost 1461 Men killd. at the Several battles & left on the field besides what were caried off, our Losses said to be between 700 & 1000 killd. & Missing but that several parties have com in Since. no News from our fleet yet.

10   was so Sick that I did not go abroad, pain in my head across my Eyes & in my Stomach & Sick at the Stomach but could get nothing to take & so woried the Day thro. about Sun Set our boat Returnd. that had been down the lake to the fleet who informs that the fleet ley at Windmill point, they Sent 18 men on Shoer to make fasheens, a small party Soon discoverd an enemy, about 40 Regulars, Canadians & Indians, who haild them & offerd Quarters which was refused, & they, our people, all got Safe into the boat, but they soon had 2 Men Killd. & 7 wounded which were Brought to the fleet, this

brought on the heavey fire from the fleet that was heard & they are yet safe. Recd. 3262 Dollars to pay of My artifficers. a Row galley came Down

11 paying of my workmen & about 3 o'clock another Row galley came Down. I had a Severe fit of Ague & fever that lasted 9 hours. about Sunset I took a Vomit that workt well & gave Some Relief, but very faint & weak.

12 Kept house had a nother hard turn of the fever & ague. Majr. Hay went down the Lake, to purchase Sauce. one Row galley is Called the Congress, the 2d Row Galley is Calld. the Trumball

13 was Very faint and had the fiver & ague again but not so hard as yesterday.

14 had a turn Of the fiver & ague this Day.

15 this Day I misst. having the ague, but was so faint that I can hardly walk, my stomack loathing all kinds of food, a little wine & water or Wine Whey being the chief of what I have taken Since Last Sabath Day. I am much better this evning but far from being well.

16 was somthing better and it is of the Lords mercy that I am alive after Such a hard & constant fatigue being out Early & late Crossing the water in the thick Fogs, that are peculiar at this place.

17 Wrote to Mr. Forbes. I was better but no relish for food. began to repair my Redoubt.

18 was better, dind at Genl. Gateses with Mrs. Hay, Col. D. Haws, Lt. Col. Pallacer and others Col. Pallicer is a Lt. Col, a Frenchman. Lt. Col. Palliceur is com up as an Assistant Engineer. we heard from the fleet that they were all safe, a desarter came in & reports that there is about 7000 Regular and other troops in Canada, they are Very Sickly espetially the forreigners, that the Inhabitants are much oppressed by them & often wish to have the Bostoniens com back again, 2 others that came of with him parted from him & are Missing.

19 Took physick, I broak out all over Very full which burnt & is Very tedious to bair, but it is probible this may be of great Service for I have been better 4 Days from the time I broak out with this Rash.

20 went a broad a little, but still unwell.

21 was poorly, went a broad but little. Majr. Hay Came home, has been down the Lake 45 Miles, brought up a plenty of Sauce for our Mess. he Says that 3/4 of all the Inhabitants in this country are Sick, such a time has not been known before.

22 I took physic, was better a good deal, feel well to what I have been.

Lt. Whitcom & 2 others brot in 2 prisoners, one Ensign Sanders of ye 29th Regt. & a Corporal, which they took a little way from St. John' towards longgale, they inform that the Regular army is Collected chiefly at the Oil Oix Noix & St. John'.

23 I was much better except the braking out.

24 I went out Dind with Genl. Bricket.

25 The Small Schooner Came up from the fleet to be refitted, She brought up 3 men that were wounded at Shanty Point by a party of Regulars that decoyd. a boat on Shore by Sending one man with his pack into the water & hailing for a boat to come & take him in, he Said he had desarted & wanted to get on bord the fleet, but the boat well mand & armd went towards the Shore with Caution, Starn foremost. the ambush was discoverd before the boat reachd. the Shoer & they soon put off & fired there Swivel & Small arms from the boat & the Schooner also fired her guns, when Several of the Enemy was seen to fall. there was a Genl. fire from the Enemy & one of our men was killed & 3 wounded. it is Said there was 3 or 400 of the Enemy in this party.

26 I went a Crosst. Independant Point to McDaniels to See the Store & Wharf & other works going on there. heard of the Battle at N. York, but the perticulars not Sertain. Majr. Pierce Returnd. Last Evng. Mr. Lucas Returnd. from Philedelphia he was at New York at the time of the Action at Long Island, & New York & brings the perticulars of the battles there. The Congress Row galley of 10 guns, besides Swivels &c Saild. down the Lake.

27 went over to Independant Point with Gen. Gates, Genl. St. Clair & Col. Trumball to view the ground for a fort to be built. afternoon wen to the Mills with Majr. Hay Supt. with Genl. Gates & St. Clair, Col. Waine, Trumball &c all in Very good Humour.

28 Drawing plans

29 I was round upon the works. Genl. Gates Genl. St. Clear & there families dind with me

30 went over to Independant Point. we heard that 3 persons was taken by the Savages from Onion River & that our people was com off & left the place. the Soldiers Confined the officers & Brought them off to Otter Creek.[101] I was drawing plans.

Octor 1 went over to the point with Col. Pallaceer to Lay out the fort. we Run Round the work but did not finish. Esqr. Gilliland came up.

2 went with Col. Pallaseer, Capt. Newland & Lt. Dallace[102] over to Independant Hill leying out the Fort agreable to a New Plan I had drawn, the Several Assistant Engineers Dind with me. I Supt. with G. Gates.

3 Genl. Gates, Revd. Dr. Gordon of Roxbury, Esqr. Gilliland & Mr. McCalley Breakfasted with me. it raind all Day. I had my Accts Settled, Recd. 518.$\frac{1}{3}$ Dollars on a Ballance of Acct. & for Service to the 30th. of Septr. Took Physick as I went to bed.

4 Laid out Som works on Independant Hill

5 Majr. Butler[103] brought in Capt. Fassit[104] & his Company Prisoners for desarting there post at Onion River[105] about 80 of them were confind in the fort for trial Joseph Wheeler Esqr Came to Lodg with me. Esqr Gilliland & Esqr McCaley keep with me.

6 I was very unwell went abroad but little.

7 Genls Gates & St Clear Col. Trumball & Lewis dind with us. we Recd the acct of about 1/4 of New Yorks being burnt. I bought 34 Gallons of Starling mediry wine brought from Albany for me at Dollars pr Gallon is of which we partook an agreeable Glass & then we had a Sociable dish of Tea which Closed the afternoon.

8 made up an Abstract for the payment of the Artificers & Recd £1372 New York Currency Equal to 3431 1/8 Dollars, Esqr Gilliland, McCalley & Watsons Dind with me. it raind & was Sloppy.

9 Paying off the workmen. a Court martial Sot for the trial of the Onion River Prisoners Genl St Clear Genl Bricket & the Pay Master Genl. dind with me. after dinner we went over to the landing to Mr. Adams, drank Tea.

10 went to the Mills & Col. Brewers Encampment bought a 34 Gallons of wine paid for it 106 1/4 Dollars, forty two pounds ten Shillings N. York money bought a Cheeney bowl for 3 Dollars of Esqr. Gilliland.

11   went over to independant point, began to Set up the pickets all was well & without fear.

12   Laying platforms in my Redoubt, the Small Schooner came from the fleet for provision & Saild down again, we heard Cannon we were allaramed by the firing of many Cannon.

13   this morning a Messinger came from the fleet about ten o'clock with a letter from Genl. Arnold informing that he had with his fleet been ingaged with the Enemies fleet 2 Day that we had lost a large Schooner run aground & burnt by the enemy a Gundalow Stript & Sunk by our men in the Bay of Bellcour our other Shipping much damaged & that we had about 60 men killed & wounded, but that we had got the better of the Enemy, but our fleet were determind to retreat to Crown point, we had this Day frequent information that our fleet was in a Shatterd Condition.   About 3 o'clock our Schooner came in Sight, Soon after a Sloop & then a nother Schooner, & then the Row Galley & after a gundalow, & they were followed by the Inhabitants from Crown point & from Panton, they were followed by Col. Hartlys Regt., part by warter & part by land, bringing all the Horses, Cattle & So forth.   at Sunset the Enemys fleet, 13 Sail anchord off about four miles from Crown point & made Signal for landing.   all the boats came up in order to take the men in to the boats, when the last accounts left

Ticonderoga Octobr. 28. 1776

This morning I visited the workmen as Upon
Usual and came in to breakfast about 8.
while I was at breakfast, the alaram Gun
was fired. about 9. O.Clock 4 boats hove
in sight. at 3 milepoint. one of the
boats of the enemy Sounded the Channel
within a Mile of our Battery at 11.o.C
we gave them a few shot. made them
Hall off again. about 17 boats how
about in sight till Sun an hour
high & then they all went off —
3 Regts came over from Independant point
the 2 Regts at the Mills. & at the landing was
order'd in. but soon after were Counter order'd

29 all was clear no appearance of the Enemy
finished the bridge a cross the Lake to
Independant point. so that men could pass

30. all was in peace. Capt. Dow & Mr. Adams
dind with me — Visited my workmen as Usual.

31. nothing material happened. I dind with
Col. Hartly Col. Waine Dr. Canada & Dr. Johnson

Novr. 1. Col. Daton came in with his Regt & a
Deserter. from Crown Point. & says that

FACSIMILE OF PAGE OF ORIGINAL JOURNAL OF COL. JEDUTHAN BALDWIN

Crown point. all the buildings at & about Crown point were burnt by our people. Some of the Inhabitants ran Some 5, Some 7 or 8 Miles in the woods with women & Children in the greatest distress, leaving all there Housel stough, Cloathing &c to the enemy, or to the flames. a Mellancholly Sight that was Seen at Ticonderoga, but we may Expect a more Mallancholly Seen to morrow or Soon. God prepair us for it & grant us a Compleat Victory over our Enemy

Octobr ye 12 & 13 our fleet Destroyed, only 5 out of 16. Returnd.

14 mounting all the Cannon we had Carriages for & all the Carpenters & Smiths making New ones, our men repairing the works & making preparation to receive the Enemy. at Evning a Flag Came from Crown point with Genl. Waterbury & 106 prison, they are on there paroll not to take up arms in the presant dispute, & to return when Calld. for. the Enemy had not landed when Genl. Waterbury came away at 10 o'clock. Mrs. Hay went for Albany with ye Baggage.

15 this Day we heard nothing from the Enemy. Capt. Rew[106] came in through the woods with 16 men, they left Genl. Waterbury Just before he Struck. went into a battoe & went on Shore.

16 I Breakfasted with Genl. Bricket. one of our Spies came in from Crown point & Says that the Enemy

were incampt. in Col. Hartleys fort & on Chimney point, about 100 tents in all & at Sunset the Enemy were landing & pitching there tents & yt he Saw a large party go out on the East Side of the Lake. he was informed that they were going up Otter Creek & to Skeensborough & Carlton said he would be in possession of Ticonderoga before Sunday & on his way to Albany where he was to have his Winter Quarters. Our Men work with life & Spirits this Day which shows a determined resolution to defend the place to the Last Extr. the habitants of the lake went of to Skeensboro 97 in No. we had 15 Tons of powder came into camp this Day & a Quantity of Lead.

17 Mounting Cannon, Making Carriages &c. Begun to make a log across the Lake or Chain to prevent the Shiping coming past the Jarsey Redoubt. it raind. Commissioner cam to this place from Congress.

18 a Very Rainey uncomfortable wet Day, I visited all the works & Redoubts & cut down part of the great bridge.

19 went to mount Hope & to the Mills. Dind with Genl. Gates &c afternoon went to Independant point, we cleard all our Guns Small arms & Cannon, Just at Sunset.

20 took the distance acrosst the Lake from the Jersey Battery & at ye point. Dind with Genl. Bricket & Mr. E Hitchcock, was out at ye Several works. Supt. with Genl. Gates, proposed making a bridge a cross to Independant Point it was aprovd. of by the Genl.

21 I visited all the Several works on this Side both in the forenoon & afternoon. in the forenoon 3 Indians that was taken with Genl. Waterbury came in, they say that 5 tribes of Indians are with the Canadian' army & are many. the 3 Stockbridge Indians left the others at Putnams Creek Last night. this evning, sone an hour high, 14 of the Enemies burch canoes came in Sight of 3 Mile point, that allarremed the army on this side. the Commissioners Set out for home. I sent 300 Dollars by Mr. John Taylor, D. Commissary, to Elisha Avery Esqr. Commissary Genl. for to be Sent to Mrs. Lucy Baldwin at Brookfield.

22 Dind. with Genl. Gates, one Man killd. & 2 taken by the Indians between the Mills & the landing. began to put ye Boom togeather.

23 it is remarkable the wind has been in the South, so that the Enemy could not come with there Vessels from Crown Point Since they came there to fight us at this place.

24 nothing material hapined this Day.

25 finish the boom acrosst & building a Bridge.

26 the 2 prisoners taken ye 22 came in from Genl. Carlton. Capt. Ayres came in with 70 Militia

27 nothing material has happined this Day, only hear of great Success at New York.

28 This morning I visited the workmen as Usual and came in to breakfast about 8, while I was at breakfast

the alaram Guns was fired, about 9 o'clock 4 boats hove in sight at 3 mile point, one of the boats of the enemy Sounded the Channel within a Mile of our Battery. at 11 o'c. we gave them a fiew Shot made them Hall of again, about 17 boats Rowd. about in sight till Sun an hour high & then they all went of. 3 Regts came over from Independant point, the 2 Regts at the Mills & at the landing was orderd. in, but soon after were Counter orderd.

29 all was clear no appearance of the Enemy, finished the bridge across the Lake to Independant point so that men could pass.

30 all was in peace, Capt. Dow & Mr. Adams dind. with me. Visited my workmen as Usual.

31 nothing material happined. I dind with Col. Hartly, Col. Waine, Dr. Canada[107] & Dr. Johnson.[108]

Novr. 1 Col. Daton[109] came in with his Regt. & a Deserter from Crown Point, & says that Carltons Army consisted of 10,000 besides 800 Canadians & Indians & that they were determind to drive us from Ticonderoga & that we might expet them to make a Vegerous push Very soon; our men were orderd to have 3 Days provision ready Cooked and to ly on there arms ready.

2 The Comtt from Congress came in. The Comtt from Mass States came in. I went round all the works with the Comtts & Genl. Officers this Day.

3   Drawing plans for the Continental States to send by the Comtt. this Evning a Scout came in & Reported that the Army had left Crown point, they went on bord the fleet yesterday about 11 o'clock, one Ship & a fiew others, boats, were in Sight.

4   this Day a Confirmation was brought in that the Enemy had left Crown Point.

5   nothing material this Day.   fair weather.

6   Making up pay Rolls for the Artificers.

7   Raisd a Barrak on Independant Point.   Lt. Evens went of to Canada with the flag commanded by Col. Wigelsworth.

8   Sent for Hay to Crown point.   fair weather.

9   fair good weather for ye Season.

10   Raisd 4 Barraks on Independant Point.   Col. Whitcomb with the officers of his Regt. did me the Honour to request me to take the Command of that Regt.   The Comtt. also gave me the offer of ye Regt. Esqr Hill Died.

11   Employed 2 Men to Cut flints geting tools for that purpose building Chimneys & Covering Barraks. Nails came in, 20 Casks.

12   Our men complaind they could not work as they had no other kind of provision but beef, flower came in afternoon.

13   began to build me a House.   fine Weather

14   cold and Snow.   raisd. Smiths Shops.
15   Col. dehaus marchd for Albany & Regt.
16   Genl. St Clair Marchchd with 5 Regts for Albana. Raisd. 2 barraks on Independant Point, some Ice on the Lake.
17   Col. Wigelsworth returnd from the Enemy at Belcove & reports that he was treated with contempt & Ill used by ye Officers.
18   Genls. Gates, Arnold & Bricket left Camp
19   Col. Paterson, Wayne, Dr. Canady & several other officers Dind. with me.   Col. Patrson Marchd off.
20   Col. Phineys Regt. Marchd. of to Albany.   200 Men geting pickets, Stoning my Seller &c.   Setled with Mr. Yancy for ye Men,   Raisd. my House at this place.

I Simon Evins Lieutnant on half pay in the Service of his britanick Majesty, having been captivated by the army of the united states of America in canada, an Inhabitant whereof I then was, & the Honourable the Congress of the Said States, having resolved that the inhabitants of Canada captivated by the united States & not taken in arms be released & Sent home (a fiew excepted) upon this condition yt they sign a parole that they will not take up arms against the united States nor give intelligence to the Enemies of Said States, I do hereby agree & promis on the Honour & faith of a Gen-

tleman that I will faithfully comply with the condition in the resolve before mentioned, contain during the war between his Brittanick majesty & Said States or untill I am duly exchanged, or discharged, I being released from my captivity & having leave to return home to Canada. Witness my Hand this 12 Day of Octobr 1776
Simon Evins

Copy

21 Over at Independant Point. I dind. with Col. Wain & Col. Wood[110]

22 it raind in the morning. onloading brick that came from Crown Point.

23 went over to independant point.

24 Recd. 141.18/ Lawfull of Mr. Yancy for Sauce.

25 Recd. 147.9.8 New York Currency to pay the workmen with that are going home.

26 paying off the men. Capt. Romanes[111] Came.

27 Drawing plans & Writing letters to inform what will be nessacery in my department next year for an army of a 10,000 Men.

28 Mrs Hay came up. Esqr. Gilliland went away.

29 went over to independant point.

30 Setled with Mr. Yancy. Making up abstract.

Decr. 1 Recd. £850-12-8 New York Currency which I this Day paid away to ye Officers.

2   Wrote to Saml. Adams Esqr & made a Return of tools & other Nessacerys wanted.   The Enemy came this afternoon to Crown Point, as Capt. Church Reports who Saw them.

3   in the fore part of this Day we were prepairing to receive the Enemy but at Evning the Ship came up to Ti and brought Pertatoes & Indian corn from Onion River to Sell, but it is only a Battoe with 3 blankets & a bedtick for Sail that Loomd up at a distance but it gave a great surprise to many.

4   Set out & went to Lake george landing.

5   Set out in ye Battoe at 6 o'clock, Called at the hunting ground by Sabbath point, breakfasted & bought 2 quarters of venison for 13/ had a Very cold Voige across the Lake, got into Fort George about x o'clock. Very Cold.   Lodgd with Mr. Carns.   the Company Majr. Stevens,[113] Majr. Frazier,[114] Dr. Canada, Capt Cristy,[115] Capt Ayres, Mr Yancy

6   Came from Fort George came down 8 M to Mr.

7   Down to Hector Mc Neals Supt. & Lodgd.

8   to Genl. Schuylers & Lodgd at Stillwater.[116]

9   to green Bush, Lodgd. at Lt Col. Fishers.[117]

10   to Albana heard the News of the Battle With our army but the Report was fals.

14   Recd. my wages to the Last of Decr., 180 Doll.

Recd at the same time 5000 Dollars by Genl. Schuylers Order to acct for

15 Writing orders to raise artificers

16 paid my sert for Express to Saratoga 24/ Left Albany at Evning. the river frose over

17 Set out from Green bush Eastward paid Expences from Ti to Albany 39/ paid at Albany & Green bush 44/ Lodgd. at Kings near the pool.

18 Dind at Whites Lodgd at Hartworth.

19 Dind at Blanford paid for expences from Greenbush to this place 20/ Lodgd. at Majr. Days W. Springfield

20 Breakfasted at Rd. Mr. Brecks at Springfield. Dind at Lt. Scotts, Palmer & Rode Home.

21 Wrote to Capt Thayr to enlist a Com of Carpen 12/ a Snowy Day

26 paid Mr Hall for the Transport of Baggage from Albany to Brookfield 88/0 Oliver Hows Expenses from Albany to Brookfield 44/ had the pleasure of Being at Brookfield from the 21 of Decr. to the 6th of January.

Jany 6. 1777 Set out from Brookfield & rode to westboro. Lodgd. at the Revd Mr. Parkmans, was strongly Invited to Brecks weding.

7 Rode to Cambridge, Lodgd at Bradishes

8 Dind with Majr. Browns & then rode to Boston, waited on Genl. Ward.

9 Majr. Chase & Majr. Brown[118] Dind with me at Moultons.

10 Dind with Genl. Ward I paid Ezekel Gould Thwait 215. 10/ Lawfull.

11 Dind. with Esqr. Gouldthwait Esqr. with a Large Company. Teems went to Ti.

12 Dind with Col. Gridley.

		Lawfull Mo.
13	paid Saml. Cookson	60. 5. 0
	paid Green & Cleverly for Tools for the Continent.	91. 11. 0
	paid Mr. John Welsh 2 Notes	23. 0. 8

Rode in the afternoon to Maldin, Lodgd at Newells Tavern.

14 Dind. at Manchester, Lodgd. at Cape Ann.

15 at the Harbour, dind. at Mr. Coffins.

16 went to Squam,[119] dind. & Lodgd. at Mr. Persons with Deacon Merrits.

17 went over to Col. Coffins, Dind. & Lodgd

18 went to the Harbour, Dind. & Lodgd. at Mr. Forbes. a Valuable prise came in.

19 went to Mr Forbes Meeting, dind at Mr. Coffins & Lodgd. Supt. with Capt. Prentice.

20 rode to Ipswich, dind With Mr. Smith, Lodgd. at Mr. Noyses with Isaacat Byfield.

21 to NewburyPort Lodgd. at Greenleaf.

22 Rode from Nubary Port to Greenland. Lodgd. at Mr. Foolsoms.
23 to Portsmouth Dind. & Lodgd. at Mr. Foolsoms
24 it Snowd & raind hard all Day.
25 Rode to Nubury Port. paid John Emery for 2000 lbs Steel £300
26 went to meeting. Dind. with Col. Ingersol. went to Church in the afternoon. Supt. & Lodgd. at Mr. Alexr Hills.
27 Rode to Salam, Lodgd at Goodhews.
28 Rode to Boston.
29 Fast Day, went to meeting paid Capt. John Harington of the armourers 100 Dollars to support his men to Albany. paid 24 Dollars for a Watch.
30 paid Majr. Chase 126. 3. 6.
    paid Mr. Stickney for Carting Steel 3. 2/.
    paid Capt. Low[120] 130 Dollars.
    & paid Lt. Emerson 130 Dollars.
    Supt. with Capt. McNeal.
31 Breakfasted with Capt. McNeal,[121] went to See his Ship. Dind. with Majr. Chase & Set out West. went to Concord, Lodgd. with Brother Saml. Parkman.
Feby. 1 to Bror. Wm. Parkman. Dind. at Westboro, Revd. E Parkmans. Lodgd. at Licester, Bro. A. Parkman.
2 Rode home to Brookfield, went to meeting afternoon.

3 at home.

4 at home.

5 at Home. Recd. a letter from Genl. Schuyler by Mr. Waite.

6 at home. Sent my Chist of.

8 Left Brookfield, lodgd. at Palmer at Mr. Scotts.

9 Rode to westfield, dind. at Mrs. Claps. to Blanford[122] Lodgd. at Peases.

10 to Tithingham[123] dind. at Brewers Lodgd. at Mansfields, Great Barrington.[124]

11 Rode to Canderhook,[125] Lodgd at ye Mills.

12 to Albany, dind. at Verners, waited on Genl. Schuyler and Col. Lewis.

13 Dind. with Genl. Schuyler. Spent the afternoon and Evning at his house with Col. Lewis, Mr. Chuyler & Mr Yates, Members of the Pro. Congress

14 Sold my Horse & Saddle for 73½ Dol. to Capt. Alexander[126] drank Tea with Docr. Stringer. Spent the Evning with Col. Hayzen. Visited the Hospitals. Recd. orders of Congress & Genl. Schuyler.

15 Breakfasted with Genl. Schuyler. Wrote to Majr. Varmonet & Capt. Marquize that there immediate presents is nessacery in this Town.

16 Majr. Vermonet & Capt. Marquize came to.

17 18 19 at albany.

20 Sent of 2 Sleys to Ticonderoga. Setled accts with ye Commissioners Recd. my Chist &c wrote to Capts Thayer, Harington & Eaton. Mrs Hay in Town. Drank Tea with Esqr. Lewis & Mrs. Hay Majr. Stevens Come in.

21 Breakfasted with Majr. Mason. Drank Tea with Colonel Hayzen. Majr. Hay come to town.

22 Setled my affairs & Sent of my Baggage & Store Sleighs & followed them in the afternoon myself. Rode to Stillwater, Lodgd at Blood Goods.

23 Sunday. Rode 15 miles to McNeals to Breakfast, to Wings to Diner & Lodgd at Blacks L. George.

24 set out at 8 o clock. Crossed 2 Very bad cracks before we got of. Foxes on ye Island. then I walked to ye Narrows with one Frost & Majr. Stevens, where we sounded the depth of the water, 7 fathoms in one place &c. and the width of the Chanel is 280 yards between ye two Islands, then rode to Sabath day point where we made a good fire, fed our horses & Eat some Vituals & then rode of in a Very great Snowstorm, wind at N. W. got to Ti about 5 o clock.

25 went over to Mount Independence, Dind & Supt with Col. Waine.

26 Visited the workmen. Rode with Col. Waine to Mount Independence & round to his house. Dind & afternoon Col. Waine, Col. Vark rode with me to the landing. Drank wine &c. Requested of Col. Wain that

men might be ordered to Saw bords with Whipsaws & that a large party might be ordered to Cut Timber for the great Bridge &c.

27 went to mount Independance the forenoon, ordered the wicker gates to be hung and the Gates Barred. by a Letter from Genl. Schuyler says that a war with France is the cause of the English requesting peace of the Americans. Col. Waine, Col. Varck & Col. Barber Drank Wine & Supt. with me. Majr. Stevens Dind. with me.

28 began to hall Logs for the Bridge.

March 1 began to build the Great Bridge, from Ticonderaga to Independant point.

2 at work at the Bridge.

3 at the bridge, Rode with Col. Waiyn to ye Mills.

4 Rode with Col. Wayne up the Creek.

5 at the bridge.

6 at ye Bridge.

7 ye Bridge.

8 Smiths came up, a fine Day at ye Bridge. Supt with Col. Wayne, 3 french Engineers Came.

9 Sunk 10 Cassoons & put down many of the posts. Col. Wayne, Mr. Adams & Lady, Dr. Mc Crey[127] & Mrs Peters Dind with us.

10 geting down the Cassoons, the Ice began to fail.

11 workt at ye Bridge, rode up East Creek.

12 Drawd. Plans for Hospital

13 began to cut timber for Hospitals, the Sleymen went off work.

14 The Ice very Roten, left working at the bridge, went over ye Mount.

15 the 3 French Engineers went off.

16 Rode over to Mount Hope & thro the woods & over the Hills West. Drank Tea at Mr. Adams with Col. Wayne, Majr. & Mrs Hays, Dr. McCray. Began the Plan of the Fort on Mount Independance.

17 Drawing plan. Raised the Roof of the Block house by Head Quarters.

18 went with Majr. Hay to the Mills in Serch of his 100£ Lost. Ephriam Potter confind. cuting timber for the hospital, went over to ye Mount.

19 Recd. a Letter from Genl. Schuyler & wrote an answer to him.

20 Capt. Low came in with 28 Carpenters.

21 puting ye foot Bridge in order across ye Lake.

22 Rode out to ye Mills & to Mr Adams. at Evening he came in after being four Days with the Enemy, he with 2 others were going to Sabath day point with 13 Horses on ye west side the Lake & were Taken by Capt. McKoy with about 18 Cocknewago Indians, about 3 o clock afternoon five miles North of Sabath day point. soon after he was taken Capt. Baldwin came along with about 25 Men from Ticonderoga going to Fort George

on the Ice. the Indians consealed themselves in ye Woods until about 3 o clock at night. Capt. Baldwin with his men passed by to Sabath Day point where they made a fire Ley down & went to sleep, when the Indians attacked them Killed 4 & took 20 which they carried off but Mr. Adams being well acquainted with Capt. McKoy, he pleading that he was only an inhabitant did not belong to the Army obtained Leave to return after marching 30

23 Capt. Eaton came in. part of Col. Robison Regt. went of. Capt. Thayer & Esqr. Winslow dind. with me. Sent a post to Albany.

24 went to mount Independance. by Capt. Peters we heard that 2 men were taken between Fort George & Fort Edward. a post went to Boston.

25 Dind. with Col. Wayne. Cold.

26 one Peer of the Grt Bridge fell to peices.

27 the Bottom of another Peer fell out.

28 Col. Wayne Dind. with us.

29 so Cold that we could not work at the Bridge. Geting Timber for ye Hospital.

30 went out to the Landing with Mrs. Hay, Col. Wayne, Mr. Stone & Majr. Hay & drank Tea with Mr. Adams. Dind. with Col. Wayne. Pleasant Day.

31 finished giting timber for 4 Hospitals. a warm Day, wind at South. Ice fails fast.

April 1 at work at ye Bridge, Raisd ye Bake House.

2 wrote to Genl. Schuyler & sent a plan of a proposed fort to be built on mount Independance, went with ye Qr. M. Genl. & laid out a large gardin at ye foot of the Mount. Col. Wayne, Majr. Rian[128] & Dr. McCray, Capt. McColey & Mrs Adams Dind. with me. a post went of to Phelidelphia.

3 a Snowey wet Day Dind. with Majr. Ryon.

4 Genl. Wayne, Col. Long,[129] Col. Mooney[130] dind with me. a cold Day.

5 went to the Saw Mills in the Morning. to Mount Independance afternoon. drank Tea at Col. Longs with Genl. Wayne.

6 Capt. Whitcom went down the Lake with 10 Men & 3 Carpenters. Capt. Nichols[131] came in. Dind. with a No. of Gentn. & Ladies at Col. Longs. warm Day

7 Majr. Stevens came up from Boston. went over to Mount Independance. Lookt out a place to hoist the provisions out of the Lake on to the Mount with a Rope & blocks. dind. with Genl. Wayne.

8 at the Bridge & among ye workmen.

9 dind at Col. Longs, & very warm Day.

10 went up East Creek with Genl. Wayne, Col. Long & Majr. Stevens, Mrs Hay &c.

11 Mrs. Hays fairwell diner to a No. of Officers.

12 got the Boom a cross the Lake. Col. Bassett[132]

went off for Willsboro[133] with 96 Men. went up to the Saw Mills with a No of Officers.

13 this Day part of Whitcombs Scout returnd, and inform that several parties of ye enemy were out this way yt they were fired upon by 3 Indians one of our men thro his hat ye Indians ran off. sent 2 Battoes down the Lake with 40 Men well armed to reinforce Col. Bassett & Bring off Hay &c. the Enemy frequently have passed from Cumberland head, 4 Brothers & to Gilliland Creek seen by ye Inhabitants. a very Rainey Day. Genl. Wayne, Majr. Stevens, Majr. Ryon, Docr. McCray & Docr. Stewert dind with us.

14 Rode to the landing with Mrs. Hay, Genl. Wayne, Col. Long, Majr. Hay & Esqr. Winslow, went to accompany her out of camp going to albany thinking it not safe to stay at this place as the Lake is now open for the Enemy & our Numbers inconsiderable by no means Equal to a body to defend this place. drank Tea Punch & wine at Mr. Adamses & live as gayly as if danger was at a distance.

15 went to mount Independance & over to the scotchmans with a No. of Officers.

16 Col. Basset Returnd. last evning without as it was Strongly guarded by the enemy.

17 went to ye mills with Genl. Wayn & Col. Long. dind. with Genl. Wayne. rainey.

18 4 of the Enemys boats 10 mils below Crown point discoverd by the raingers Col. Basset & 100 men went down the Lake well armed. Mrs. Peters went down with her Child.

19 4 Indians fired at by the sentry at the Mills last night. at work at the Bridge, Block housen & Laying Platforms. dind. with Majr. Stevens.

20 went to the mills & to mount Independance.

21 one of the piers of the Bridge turnd. over.

22 went over Mount Prospect & down to the mills. Col. Bassett returnd. from Crown point with 20 Tons of Hay & 2 Load faciens & 2 small cannon left by the regulars last year. dind. with Genl. Wain, Genl. Patersons & others. Col. Brewer came in with Col. Carlton.

23 Col. Marshal[134] & Col. Francis[135] came in. went in the berge with Genl. Wayne, Genl. Paterson, Col. Long & Majr. Stevens up 3 Miles towards Skeensboro after Veal. dind. at Capt. Levensworths[136]

24 raisd. the fraim for the Crane on the edge of the Mount for hoisting up whatever may be wanted on Independance. Dind. at Col. Longs with all ye Field officers.

25 The Field & Genl. officers Dind. at our House. Gen. Wayne orderd to ye Southward. One of Col. Martials men had his hand blown of by his gun bursting. Dr. Johnson came up.

26 all the Field officers Dind. at wallises Tavern & Supt. ye Entertainment given.

27 Dind. at Genl. Waynes. a Very Rainey D

28 a field Day. Dind. at Genl. Waynes. a scout went down the Lake. went to the Sawmills with the Comp drank Tea Syllebub &c.

29 Crosst. the Lake to Fort George with Genl. Wayne & Drs Johnson & Rosse

30 Genl. Wayne left Fort George.

May 1 a Rainey Day, wind at North.

2 at Fort George. almost Sick with the cold I got crossing the Lake. I kep at Head Quarters with Col. Van Dyck,[137] Supt. with the Officers & Docrs. at the Hospetals.

3 Set of with Dr. Johnson abot 8 o'clock this morning had the wind a head stopt at fox or 14 miles Island & at 18 mile Island, high wind taried untill about Sunset when the wind abated, we set off again & got up to the Landing a little before sunrise. discoverd Indian fires on the mountains below Rogerses Rock,[138] I almost Sick with a cold.

4 Returnd. to Ticonderoga, was bled in the arm. Genl. Paterson, Col. Long, Marshal & Francis Dind. with us.

5 laid out the ground for the Hospital. field Day. afternoon I was better

6 went to the Mills with Genl. Paterson. a Block house ordered to be built near the North mill on the Hill. Capt. Whitcom discovered 16 Indians 4 miles S. W. of the mills

7 a Wet Day. Genl. Paterson, Col. Francis, Docr. Stodard & Capt. Raymond dind. with me.

8 a Rainey Day. heard of Indians on ye Lake.

9 Laid out & began a Redout between the french lines & ye old fort on high Ground.

10 Carpenters left work at ye Bridge & went to driving a frieze round the front of the french lines. a scout went down ye L-

11 began the Redout on ye Hill at ye french lines. 13 Tories brought in.

12 Examining the Tories. Dr. Potts, Col. Kosi-. osko[139] & Col. Wilkinson[140] came in. 2 Tories brot in.

13 Examining 15 Tories that were taken in Arms near Otter creek below Crown Point; Viz. Simpson, Jenny, Benja Cole, Edward Simmons, John Hart, Saml. Philips, Nathl. Corbin, Aaron Cole Junr., Joseph West, Wm. West, Aaron Cole Senr., David Cole, John John Philips, John Martyn all of and belonging to the New hampshire grants. After a long & cross Examining 6 of them Acknowledged there whole Plot & informd of 12 others that were knowing to & advising them to go to St. Johns to Join the Regular Army. Dr. Potts & Col.

Kosiosko Lodg with us. Dind. at Genl. Patersons. went to ye Mills.

14 Viewd. the Lines. at work on ye Redouts. a fine Day. we heard that the Naval Store & Provision Magazine at St. Johns were lately burnt, if this be true we shall not soon be attack. Heaven fights for us to prevent our distruction. Genl. Paterson with a No. of Gentn. Dind. with me.

15 went round the lines with Lt. Col. Kosiosko. Col. Hay went to skeensboro.

16 wrote to genl. Gates & Col. Stewart. Genl. Paterson, Cols. Francis, Wilkins, Kosiosko & Majr. Hull[141] Supt. with me. Dind with Majr. Stevens, was round the works, Col. Bellows came in with the malitia. drawing plans of ye Hospital & the works at Fort George & Sent them down to Genl. Gates. Rainey Day.

17 went round to the works on this side and on Mount Independance Dind. with Dr. Potts. a Showry Day.

18 this morning Capt. Stone brought in 2 prisoners both belonging to the New hampshire grants, one of them late from Canada & confirms the Acct. of ye Genl. House & a Store being burnt & that the enemy are building one 20 gun Ship at St. Johns. Col. Hay came home.

19 Raisd. the flagstaff on Mount Independance.

20 Genl. Poor Came in with 600 Men.

21 went round the work with Genl. Poor.

22 a large fatigue party at the French lines. Dind. with Docr. Potts & ye Genls.

23 at the works on the french lines & at Mt Independance. Genl. Paterson & Col. Kosiosko went to Skeensboro. Majr Ayres came in.

24 Majr. Ayres & Capt. Wilcott[142] Joind. my works as Assistant Engineers. Genl. Poor Rode with me to ye Mills. Coll. Marshall, Dr. Stodard & Majr. Ayer dind. with me. a fine pleasant Day.

25 the boom & Bridge in a heavey gale of wind gave way & with some difficulty they were brought back to place.

26 On Mount Independance a good part of this Day. Esqr. Winslow viewd my acct. I bught a Horse for 110 Dollars.

27 Raisd the Hospital N. side & a Store. Dind. with docr. Johnson.

28 a scout Returnd. from Split rock (Lt. Liford[143]) & says that the Enemy was there with two Vessels 7 Gunboats & about 40 Battoes. Exspresses wer sent immediately to albany to berkshire & to No. 4 & Capt. Whitcomb down the Lake to watch the motions of the Enemy. began another redout on the high ground N. W. from the fort in ye rear of ye french lines.

29 work at ye Bridge Anchoring of ye Boom & geting Logs for it. Laid out a Redout to ye Left between

ye old fort & french Lines part of Capt. Whitcombs Scout came in & inform that the Enemy fired yesterday about 80 Cannon, besides a Number of Volleys of Small arms at & near the Split rock.

30 Recd. 9,000 Dollars, paid of my workmen. had 10 Cannon come from Lake George. Mrs. Tucker kep at our house, came from Skeensboro. at Evning Capt. Whitcom came in & reports that the Enemy was gone back from Split rock down ye Lake.

31 Rode to the Mills & round to the workmen. in the afternoon to Mt. Independ.

June 1 Rode to the Landing & paying of my workmen. Rote to Genl. Gates.

2 Dind. with the Surgeons on ye Mount.

3 Agreed for 20 Brickmakers & 16 masons & 40 Shingle Makers.

4 paying of my workmen, brickmakers began to work. Lt. Emerson Discharged.

5 Rode to the Mills & to ye Landing with Genl. Paterson, Col. Long & Hay.

6 Col. Kosiusko came up from Albany.

7 Rode over Mount independance. Laid out long lines between the redoubts that I hope will never will be finished as they are Staked now.

8 went round among the workmen in the morning & to crown point with Genl. Paterson, Col. Kosiusko, Dr.

Crague & Docr. Majr. Armstrong[144] & 30 men measured the width acrosst to Chimney point 400 yards & the Chaniel in the deepest place 56 feet water for about 100 yards wide & then grows shallower gradually on both sides.

9 came home in ye morning dind with the Doctors at ye Hospital.

10 went to ye Hospital forenoon. dind with Genl. Paterson & a large company of Officers at Genl. Poors headquarters.

11 Rode to the Mills & over to ye Mount.

12 Genl. St. Clair came in. 2 prisoners brot in from Canada, they say the enemy will in fact be here in about a fortnight 10,000 Strong.

13 went round the works with Genl. St. Clair. it raind hard the most of ye Day.

14 went with Genl. St. Clair over & round Mount Independance. movd the floating Bridge to the loer side of the Peers. in the afternoon went with Col. Kosiusko to advise what works had best be done on the mount. drank Coffey with ye Genl.

15 ordered to Skeensboro to order the works repaird at that place. went up in Company with Capt Fisher & Mrs. Tucker. Lodgd with Capt. Lonson.

16 Layd out the lines for a new Fort, the old one all to be taken down. Lodgd at Govenor Skeens Seat.

17 began the work of the new fort. Dind with Mrs. Tucker, Capt. Lonson, Capt. Fisher and the Chaplain of Col. Warners Regt. Mr Allen. went into ye Publick fields.

18 Left Skeensboro at 8 o'clock morning. Dind at $\frac{1}{2}$ way spring. wind ahead. Stopt at 6 miles point, met the Schooner & Gundola going up to Skeensboro. heard that the Indians had taken 2 of our people & killd four others & wounded three more. the 2 first taken & 2 killd were betwen the French lines & the bridge. yesterday, two more killd & 3 wounded about half way to Crown point, a party of Raingers.

19 Genl. Schuyler came in. this morning breakfasted with ye Genl. Capt. Whitcom cam in & brot an Indian scalp, saw where 2 others had been halld away after they were killd.

20 a scout returned from Crown point they discovired near 5 mile point the tracks of about 30 of the enemy & saw 2 indians which they fired at but they being at two great a distance they made there escape. began the works at 3 places on Mt. Independance. I dind with a large Company at ye Hospital.

21 went over the Mount & round the works with Genl. Schuyler & St. Clair & movd som cannon from Ty to the mount south wharf the Genl. Officers & a number of others dind with us.

22 Genl. Schuyler went off for Fort George. afternoon I rode to the Landing. Drank Tea with mrs Adams.

23 dind with Genl. Poor, went onto the mount with Genl. St. Clair proposed to make a Laboratory of the old Hospital. a scout came in from Onion River & says that the enemy are incamped at Gillilands in a great No. of Tents the Indians very thick they took one of his party & the rest but Just made there escape & that the Enemy would soon be at Ty with there army & 9 Vessels besides Gunboats battoes &c. &c.

24 the regulars came to Crown Point.

25 the Artificers passed muster. alaremed with indians.

26 one man killd & another scalped by the indians between the Mills & the landing. paid 103. 14. 3 for wine, Shugr, Cheese, Coffey & Chocolat. worked at the bridge & Breastworks.

27 leying platforms on the batteries on the S. E. side the Mount & driving piles acrosst the E creek carrying stores over to the mount.

28 the Enemy incamped at putnams point & 4 Vessels on this side. 3 men came in & report that by information from one of the Inhabitants the enemy are 8000 regulars, 1500 Canadians & Indians, that they had near a 1000 Tents pitched. by a nother person from Otter

creek that 500 are gone up that way & was last night within 8 miles of Rutland, where we have a considerable store belonging to N. H.r

29 a large Quantity of provision brot from the landing Lake George left only about 25 barrels of pees & flower there. moving our Magazines to the Mount.

30 early in the morning the Enemy appeared at 3 mile point with 18 Gunboats & a fiew other boats landing about 300 men that marched up to the mills to the bridge & in front of the Breastwork but were soon drove back. this afternoon two large Ships appeared, one 20 guns & the other a 16 gun Ship & 2 tenders they warped up in a line with the Boats across the lake from 3 mile point & made a formidable appearance.

July 1 a Reinforcement came to the Enemy, about 41 battoes & landed on the East side, where they incamped, & the enemy incamped this Day at 3 Mile point. landed there artillery & throwing up works on both sides. a considerable firing at the mills, but no mischief done. this morning 2 expresses came across lake george with good news from G. Washington, that the Enemy was flying on which account we had a Fu. d' Joy at 12 o clock fired 13 Cannon &c.

2 a large reinforcement came to the Enemy, about 1 o clock they attacked our lines after driving in our piquet of which they killed one Lieut. of warners, 4 privats &

wounded 11 others. the Enemys Loss not known. this morning the block house & Mill burnt and the party got in Safe. the Enemy all round us & very bold firing away.

3 the enemy throwing up one battery in front of ye french lines. a move in front of the Jersey battery across the water & very peacible all day. Took down ye Block house on the Mount & began a Magazine. Col. Bellows[145] Came in with 800 Men & 80 head of Cattle besides Sheep, a fine reinforcement at this Time when we are surrounded by our enemy, which I pray God may be Scattered.

4 puting up the Block house, moving som Cannon, laying platforms & prepairing for the Seige, the enemy Numerous & bold.

5 the Enemy appeared on the Mount above on the S. W. opening a Battery, a large Ship came up. a high wind at N. the Enemy made a disposition of an attack but were prevented by the high wind or from some other motive, but now appeared to be in readiness to open there Batteries. about 10 o clock at night. a Speedy retreat was ordered and the main boddy of the army got off From Ty & Mount Independance a little before Sun rise followed by the Enemy but did but little damage.

6 Marched thro' the woods to Castleton,[146] dind at Shermons, Hobbleton. Lodgd at Castleton where the Enemy had killd Capt. Williams we took 8 prisoners out

of a party of 500 Canadians and Regulars & about 40 cattle.

7 in the morning a heavey fire in the rear for some time near an hour a heavey battle, but as the rear consisted of the feeble part of the army they, after an obstinate resistance were obliged to give way to superior numbers. the body of the army Marchd to Rutland. dind at Col. Meedses where we were Joind by a No. of Col. Warners Men & those that had been in action. Just at night we marched to a Very woody place the inhabitants gone.

8 Very Rainey Afternoon and night.

9 Marcht between the Mountains to arthington left Col. Warner at Manchester.

10 Marched 20 Miles to Bro.

11 had men Died on the road. we lodgd Near salatoga a Very wet afternoon & night. many of our men ley in the woods without fire or covering. many Sick.

12 went to fort Edward. Genl. Nixon[147] with his Briggade came to Fort Edward the Artificers ordered to Saratogo. I lost all my baggage at Skeensboro with my papers with 6491 Dollars of Publick money & left destitute of a second Shirt, stockings or breeches to change my linen. the long & fatigueing march of 110 Miles thro the woods has brought me Very dirty & uncomfort-

able, all the Artillery, Stores & Provisions & Baggage of all kinds Lost.

13 Rode to Moses Creek & round thro the woods With the Genl. Officers. Retured to Fort Edward.

14 Recd 5000 Dollars at Fort Edward. went to Saratoga to direct the workmen in mounting the Cannon, got the Carpenters & Smiths to work, with as great expidition as possible. dind at McNeals ye 15th.

15 with the workmen getting tools. Lodgd at Mr. Niffs Lt. Hitchings[148] went to Albany for Armourers Tools to go to Fort Miller.

16 at Saratoga with ye workmen. Fort George Evacuated.

17 went to fort Miller. Genl. Schuyler, St Clair & others came to Saratoga.

18 they went back to Fort Edward.

19 Making carriages, Wheels &c. 6 pair of bellowses came from Albany with Lt. Hitchings. Genl. Fellows[149] went down.

20 at home all Day.

21 went to McNeals, sent to Boston for a Number of articles the one 1/2 of the Albany Militia sent home. Began the Smiths shops by ye Genls bought 6lbs of Loaf Shugr for 9 Dollars & 20 3/4 lbs of Cheese for 10 3/4 Dollars & one 1/4.

22 with the workmen in the forenoon, dind with

Dr. McCrey at Mr. Lansings. afternoon I Rode to Fort Miller & Moses Creek & back to Saratoga. the artillery came Down by order to Saratoga. Col. Brown went to genl. Schuyler with advice of an attack at Fort Stanwix.[150] Genl. Arnold went up to Fort Edward. Blazing Hot with death in the pot.

23 Fort Edward evacuated & destroyed by our peoples & retired to Moses Creek. yesterday a Scirmish happined between Genl. Nixons Piket & a party of the enemy in which we had 5 Men killd & 8 men wounded. Col. Nixon' Horse Shot under him. the Corps of Artillery came down to Saratoga with the Powder.

24 Raised a Smiths Shop at Saratoga two Men one Lieut. & a privat killd of Genl. Lerneds Brigade. many families moving.

25 with the workmen at Saratoga.

26 Recd. orders to march with 30 Carpenters to head Quarters Moses Creek. 4 Men & one Woman killed near Fort Edward & cut to peices in a most inhuman manr.

27 went to Moses Creek with Capt. Lows Carpenters crossed the River to the W side. went back to Saratoga at evning.

28 went up to Moses Creek in the Morning. Genl. Learnard & Genl. Innbrook retreated back to camp. one man killd & scalped by 2 indians within 20 rods of the guard.

29 Rode with the Genls. to the several incampments. 2 Men killd at Fort miller one of Col. Nixons Sentrys killd. heard that the enemy arivd yesterday at Fort George with 27 Boats & a large sail coming up by the narrows.

30 went to Fort Miller with the army. the Enemy crossed the river to the west side 300 & attack the rear of our army killd one Soldier, wounded one Lt. Mortally & 4 privates were wounded. the Loss on the enemys side not known but supposed to be 10 killd.

August 1 getting down Rafts of Bords &c. &c. the enemy appear'd in several places, lurking indians, they killd 3 men Scalpt two in sight of camp on the East side the river.

2 Genl. Glover & Col. Wiglesworth[151] came up. Sent of most of the Cannon &c.

3 had several men killd, 5, & wounded, 7, & one man scalped, 2 officers & 6 soldiers taken. took a prisoner. Retreated at 6 o clock afternoon with all our Stores & bagage, Cut away & burnt 9 large Bridges. 2 tories taken with Genl. burgoins pass from Skeen. & back.

4 getting up Stores, mounting Cannon & geting Smiths to work. a Very rainey day got into Stillwater 10 o clock in the Morning. Cut & burnt 4 large bridges on the road this morning as we came in

5 All the Carpenters at work geting up ye Stores.

6 All the smiths at work at 13 fires. moving of Baggage & Stores to Half moon. sick sent of to Albany.

7 Sent of 80 bb of powder (yt is 10 Ton) to albany. Genl. Schuyler Wt to Treat with the Indians at Albany. Col. Longs Regt. marched of to A. for Discharge.

8 a majr. & 2 boys taken. Majr. Van Varter Killd, one man killd a capt. wounded, one Indian killd & scalped by our scout. sent of the heavey peices of cannon to half moon with other stores.

9 the Artificers went with there Tools & Baggage to Albany. Oliver went with my Wagon to Half Moon.

10 Genl. Schuyler & St. Clair ordered to Congrs the sick all sent of geting the stores to 6 mile point. by a desarter & a prisoner we hear that the main body of the enemy are at Fort ewand & there flying camp at Fort Miller & are to move to Saratoga next wednesday. 7 tories taken.

11 News of fort Stanwix being invested & a surver Battle fought 6 miles below. Genl. Harriman wounded & 14 field officers killd & wounded on our Side. the Enemy Loss 50 Indians killed & left on the field with 100 others of the enemy. Genl. Harriman recovrd the field, buried the Dead brought of the wounded & retired Back.

12 Genl. Learnard Marchd with 3 Regts viz. Balies, Vanshoiks & Jacksons for Fort Stanwix. Genl. St. Clair

left Camp for Philadelphia, Genl. Lincholn[152] came to camp from ye Grants.

13 the heaviest part of the stores carried off. Genl. Arnold went of for F. Stanwix.

14 Genl. Schuyler with Genl. Glovers Brigd marched for half moon. at 2 o clock P. M. a scout came in & reported that the enemy was advancing within 6 miles, mending Bridges &c. also heard that 1500 of the enemy was marched for Cambridge in the grants Genl. Lincoln set out for the grants. a Very Hot Day. Lent Col. Hay 650 Dollars.

15 went with the army to 6 miles point. Lodgd at Abram Forts House.

16 this morning I was ordered up to Stillwater with 280 Men to burn the Bords left cut & burn the Bridges & Break up the Roads after we had got the teems Loaded with some stores &c. that had been left. at Stillwater about 1 o clock we discovered 2 men with packs crossing the river from the uper to the loer Island. a Serjt & 6 men went over to discover who they were, one of the men returnd & said there was a considerable No. incamped on the Island. I immediately sent 50 Men well armd on to the Island to take the party, & bring them off, while the Rest of the Body ley on there arms ready to assist if nessciery. in about one Hour Some of my party of 50 returnd with 4 Men. Several women & chil-

dren in a Canoe they had picked up, (for they waided across the River to get on to the Island). the whole party of tories taken on the Island is 4 Men, 7 Women & 17 Children, 28 in all. it took 3 hours to get them all over with there baggage, as the water was wide & run swift, which all came safe into camp, after executing the orders I was sent upon. those tories are persons of welth Inhabitants of Stillwater who had secreted there Houselstough, Cloathing & movables in the woods & then went on to this desolate Island that was thick wooded where they designd to Remain till our Army was movd down & then they would return home under the protection of Burgoin. these Tories are

John Jeffers, his wife & 3 small children	5
Benja. Burrows, his wife & four Children	6
John Vice, his wife & four Children	6
Thos. Jeffers Jun. & wife & four Children	6
Mrs Mageer & one Child	2
one Negro Woman & 2 Children of Jefferses	3
in all	28

17 it raind in the Morning. heard that the famous Capt Butler with 28 men were taken by our Army at ye Mohawk River. all our heavey Stores movd down to ye Island.

18 I marched with Genl. Poors Breggade, Crossed

the Mohawk River at Lowdens ferry, afternoon dind in the woods on fryd Chickens, Cold Beef &c. we incamped the Briggade near Mr Canoots.

19 Rode up the river to the ferries & several fords across the River. below. Dind with Genl. Poor, afternoon Rode to Van Schoiks Island head Quarters, Lodgd at New Sity, Dr Bartletts Had the acct of the Victory gaind by Genl. Starks near Benington 936 Killd & taken. Genl. Gates came to Camp this evning.

20 Rode to Albany dind with Mrs Hay & afternoon Rode to Genl. Poors Camp above the Qohoes Lodgd & Breakfasted. Genl. Schuyler left Camp this morning.

21 Rode with Genl. Poor & Col. Wilkison to head Quarters Van Schoiks Island.

22 at Van Shoiks Island geting the Smiths to work. 60 Carpenters sent for. Govenour Clinton[153] with 1500 Militia came to camp. Col. Briewer came from Binington with 45 Tories taken in Battle.

23 the Carpenters of Capt. Thayers & Lows companies came up from Albany. Col. Courtlands & Col. Livingstons Regt marched for Fort Stanwix.

24 a Number of Tories taken & brought to camp & sent to Albany & Down the Country. 4 Desarters hessians Came to camp by the way of Benington. Just at Evning Capt. Goodell[154] of Brookd Brought in 4 prisoners that he had taken, (with his small party of 6 men),

at Saratoga, where the enemy have a camp of about 1500 on the East of the River & have sent a large party to fort Stanwix.

26   went to Albany.

27   at Albany. got Cloth for a Suit of cloaths out of the store.   I left my Accts with the Commissioners.

28   went up to camp, Van Schoiks Isle troops came up from Coneticut.

29   Set 20 men making coal on ye Isle.

30   Rode with Genls. Gates, Arnold & Paterson to Dine with Genl. Poor.

31   in Camp a Day of Ease.

Sept'r 1   Genl. Lincholn came to Camp with Ginl. Palmer & Docr Taylor. a flag of Truce came this Evning from Genl. Burgoin with a letter for Genl. Gates & another letter to Genl. Gates from Genl. Frazier. several prisoners brot into camp.

2   Rode up to Genl. Poors Camp, dind with him in Company with a Comtt from New Hampshire & then to Camp & then to Albany. Supt & Lodgd with Dr. Potts. left my watch to be cleand with Mr Abbt. Sent a Tick to Mrs hay No 58 m 255, No 55. 107.

3   in Camp

4   in Camp. Rode round the Island, went to Albany at evning. Lodgd.

5   went up to camp after buying 400 bords.

6 at camp. went up to the Cohoes to the mills, got 6 loads plank of M. Lansing.

7 in camp all day. a New suit of cloaths Brought me. Loaded my wagons for a march, 20 wagons with tools & baggaig.

8 marcht with the whole body of the army to the Mills. the Front at Dow Fondays.

9 Marched in the Front with the Carpenters & pionears. Col. Morgans[155] Riflemen the advanced party & flanks got to Stillwater about 12 o clock & at 2 o clock began a bridge a Cross the River. afternoon a flag Came in with a Doctr from Burgoin to Visit the Wounded Hessians & Regulars at Benington. a prisoner sent home.

10 a wagon Came with the bagage of the prisoners & 3 Servts to those taken at Bennington & went on.

11 making Bridges & cutting cross Roads to advance in Collums. orders for a March.

12 Struck tents at gun firing & marcht the whole army before Sunrise. incamped upon the high Ground above Beemis's, 3 miles from Stillwater. 800 of Genl. Starks crossed the River to Stillwater & incamped there.

13 5 prisoners taken at Saratoga, they Say that Burgoin marches to meet us this Day with his whole army Collected & that Genl. Lincoln is at Skeensborough.

14 Genl. Starks came to camp from Benington, the enemy Crossed the River at Saratoga.

15 the Enemy advanced to Van Varters Hill.

16 4 prisoners brot in Capt. Lane & Capt. ——— came in with a flag.

17 the people work with hig spirits. Dind with Doct Potts & Genl. Gates &c. Lent Genl. Gates 40 Dollars for a French Capt. going to Cohos yesterday.

18 Genl. Arnold marched out to meet Genl. Burgoin in the woods, but no action hapned.

19 about one o clock our left piquet fell in with a large party of the enemys light troop, a heavy fire lasted 3/4 ov an hour, both parties was strongly reinforced, at last we drove the enemy above a mile took a No. of prisoners & there wounded which were brought in. About 1/2 after 3 o clock we discovered the Enemy Marching up in heavey Collums against our left wing. Several Regts was immediately ordered to meet them, a heavey fire soon began and lasted without intermission until half an hour after Sunset, our army several times drove the Enemy & once took a field peice, for want of Amunition it was lost. many kill & wounded on both sides among the dead is Lt. Col. Coburn & Lt. Col. Adams, two Very brave Officers.

20 this morning 112 Indians came to Camp, the Enemy keep the field of Battle so that we did not attempt to bury our dead.

21 it was reported that the Enemy was approaching to attack us & then soon after that they were retreating

but neither provd true. Recd the news of Col. Browns being at Ty, fired 13 Cannon & gave a genl. Whooray throo all our camp. 2 tory prisoners taken by ye Indians.

22 Genl. Lincoln came to camp. 2 british soldiers taken & one Scalp by the Indians. Genl. Gates gave 20 Dollars for each Prisoner but would give nothing for the Scalp. a wet Day, I sick with a bad cold. the Prisoners just brot in say that they lost, in the action of ye 19th, 700 men.

23 the Camp allarmed All hands at work, 10 prisoners brot in & som desarters.

24 All the baggaige loaded in the morng and Sent of in consequense of intellig that Burgoin would attack us this day at 10 o clock. a considerable No. of malitia came in & Genl. Lincoln came in with 1680 men at night. by the Returns there was in the acton of the 19 Killd

	Lt. Col.	Capts.	Subs	S.	C.	D.	Privat
	2	3	2	3	0	2	51
Wound	0	6	15	13	0	1	182
missing	0	1	1	7	0	0	29

262
56

318

25   this morning we took one prisoner & killd 8 of the Enemys picket.

26   took 16 prisoners in several parties & 2 scalps, yt the Indians brot in 30 indians went of this Day.

27   this morning one of our prisoners desarted from the Enemy & a prisoner brot to camp. the greatest part of the Indians went of home.

28   took 2 Scalps & 11 prisoners & desarters.

29   the Brookfield Volenteers came up.

30   made a Raft on Battoes to cary our Wagons across the River.

Octobr 1   went to View the Enemys camp & reconoiter there lines & Guards. Col. Brown came from Ty & Lake George where he had taken 315 british Prisoners, Including 15 Officers, 5 of which were Capts & retook 110 of our prisoners. Destroyed 200 Battoes, 17 armed Gondaloes & one Sloop, mounting carriage Guns & destroyed a No. of Carriages & Canon & brought of 10,000£ Value in plunder.

2   three prisoners taken & three hessn desarters came in from the Enemy, took 7 Horses from the Enemy & at Evning 24 prisoners brot in from the east side the River & a Capt. 2 Subs & 10 men & 40 Horses & cattle brot in on the west side the River taken at Saratoga. bought a Horse & a mare.

3   four Hessian Desarters came to us with there arms

& acoters took 4 Horses from the enemy & a yok of oxen. ye prisoners went to Albany.

4   2 british Soldiers desarted to us. we were allarmed by the Enemys crossing the River with there Wagon &c. a forraiging they soon returnd.

5   this Day 14 Prisoners & desarters brot to our camp & 7 Horses, oxen, Cattle & Sheep about 30, & 16· Swine.

6   prepaird 5 battoes for fire Rafts.

7   went to albany with Dr. Pots. at one O clok the Enemy came out against our left Picket. we met them in the woods & drove them into there lines & from Some of there works took 6.6 pounders & 2 12lb all brass & there impliments, Tints, Kettels, Baggage wagons, Ammunition &c. with 200 officers & Soldiers taken Prisoners. our loss Genl. Arnold wounded in the leg, Majr. Lithgow[156] wounded in the arm & many others Killd & wounded

8   went to Camp before noon a fireing upon the enemy 24 Hessians came to us 189 Prisoners Sent to Albany.

9   a Very wet Day out a making Bridges the Enemy left there Camp at Gunfire & marched. I went with Genl. Nixon to there Camp, found they had left Sick, wounded & Nurses. took 2 Ammunition wagons, one cas of Medicine. found a No. of the Enemies Horses dead on the road & there baggage left.

10   Marched to Saratoga with the Army took a large Quantity of Provisions & a Consider No. of Prisoners &c.

11   Took the Enemies Boats & provisins & 60 prisoners besides desarters.   Making Bridges on the Road.

12   building Bridges across Schuylers Creek in 2 places. a large No. of prisoners & Desarters came in this Day.

13   Building Bridges rode with Genls Nixon & Glover to propose works &c.

14   a flagg came from Burgoin by his Ajut. G. at Eleven o clock A. M., a sesation of arms was agreed to until sunset for proposals of an accomidation which Genl. Burgoin desired Genl Gates to make. they were sent in by our A. Genl. 5 o clock P. M about 60 prisoners & desarters brot in.

15   a flag came out with proposals of a small alteration of the 6th article which was consented to, after several conferences, but somthing still remained with respect to commissarie & Staff officers, the Capitulation was not finished untill after sunset, a desisive answer was to be given at ten o clock to morrow Morn. 50 Indians & tories taken above Fort Edwd.

16   in the morning Genl. Burgoin wrote to Genl. Gates yt he had heard large detachments were sent from our Army & he requested yt 2 of his officers might come & see the truth of ye report the Letter was sent back

with a message that if the the agreement was not signd & sent in Immediately hostilities should Commence at 12 o clock.

about 3 o clock P. M. the Articles of Capitulation were brought out signed by John Burgoin Lt. Genl. all our army ordered to ly on their arms & Guards doubled as of late has been usual.

17 About 11 o clock A. M. the enemy laid down there arms & Marched out thro our Army the most agreeable sight that ever my eyes beheld. Burgoins Army that capitulated were 6000 & of them 2448 were British. Genl. Nixon' Briggade marched for albany the British army for New city.

18 This Day the main boddy of the American army marched to Albany 36 M, this forced march was ocationed by our hearing that the Enemy was coming up the River & had burnt Esopus.

19 at Albany, the Troops much fatigued.

20 at Albany mending the roads down the west side the River 14 Miles.

21 Rode down on the East side the River as far as Stotack.[157]

22 Genl. Poors Brigade Marched.

23 at Albany Capt. Low came down.

24 at Albany Capt. Thayer came down.

25 Genl. Burgoynes baggage Sent over the River.

Genl. Larneds Briggade marched down on the west Side the River. Col. Morgan Marched the same way. Genl. Gates & family dind with us. Supt. at Tuttles laid out the Park.

26 Went to meeting all Day.

27 a Very Wet Day Genl. Burgoyne & other of his officers left Town with Genls. Glover & Whipple for Boston.

28 a great rain I was blooded.

29 it continewed raining, I took a Vomit. Drew plans for Barracks & Store housen.

30 Kept House myself Glovers & Batersons Brigades Marched of to Quemans[158] & went some by Water

31 went to the Mills. Genl. Nixons Briggade wint into Quarters in Town.

Novr 1 Rode with Genl. Gates to Queemans 4 Barraks to be built there, 250 feet long each, the mills set to work.

2 Rode with Genl. Paterson & Col. Brewer to Kinderhook.

3 went at Albany with Genl. Paterson.

4 admited to an Honble Assembly.

5 went to Van Vasters Mill, bought 2650 Bords for the Labratory Store.

6 at albany, Sent after Coal.

7 four Brigades ordered down to the Southward.

8 Dind at Docr Potts ye Smiths left work.
9 went to meeting.
10 at albany, it Raind all Day.
11 getting my wagon ready for a Journey. Bought a Span of Horses for 10£
12 Recd into a Society as a Craftsman.
13 Set out from Albany for Brookfd. Rode 10 miles Lodgd at Lorubecks at Scotack.
14 Rode to Mr. Coals at Nobletown Lodgd
15 Rode to Kellogs Nortans at Lowdonton Lodgd.
16 Rode to Springfield Lodgd at Rev. Mr. Brecks.
17 to Brookfield Lodgd with Mrs. Baldwin. & you may guess for ye Rest.
18 at home.
19 at home & at home the remainder of the month.
Decr 1 at home

Genl. Burgoins Return of his Army, Octobr 17, 1777. Since the Evacuation of Ticonderoga, The Killed, Wounded & Prisoners,

British by Capitulation	2442
Foreigners by Do	2198
Sent to Canada	1100
Genl. Burgoyn & Staff among which are 6 membrs of Parlmt	12
Sick & wounded	1126
Prisoners of war before the Surrender	400

Desarters 300
Lost at Benington 1220
Killed between the 17 of Septr & 18 of Octobr 600
Taken at Ticonderoga 400
Killed at Genl. Harrimans Batl 300

10098

39 Brass Cannon Royals & Morters and impliments and Stores compleat

5000 Stands arms.

400 Setts harness.

a number of Amunition Waggons and harness.

6 field pieces at Benington.

2 Do & 4 Royals at Fort Stanwix.

Brass Ordinance.

2   24 pounders
4   12   Do
1   9   Do
19   6   Do
6   3   Do
2   8 inch Morters
5   Royals

39

July 6th 1778 Recd the perticular acct of the Battle of ye 28th in ye Jerseys viz Our Loss is 7 officers & 52 R & file K. 17 officers & 120 Rank & F wounded. The Enemys loss is 245 R & F found dead on the field & four Officers. Col. Monkton. There wounded is 1255. Desarted since they left Philadelphia 1572, taken prisoners 117

7 Rode the Grand Rounds With the Field officers of the Day to Dobses ferry to the several guards in front, dind with Genl. Morris at Genl. Gateses afternoon rod to Rye to Marrineck[159] & Returnd at evning. a Very hot Day.

8 Genl. Gates, Nixon, Morrice and others dind with me. a Battoe taken by ye galleys.

9 rode to Tarry Town in the Morg & back to Camp & at evning rode back to Tarytown & to Croton ferry.

10 rode to Kings ferry to peeks kill to Crompon to Northcastle[160] dind at Benja. Kipp to Head Quarters. a Frigate of 36 guns & 2 Row galleys went up to Kings ferry, 2 cannon went up to K. ferry.

11 Genl. Nixon' Briggade Incamped on the right of Mount defiance.

12 I went to Tarry Town the Tarter frigate fired briskly at us. Genl. Clinton & Morrices Briggd incamped on Mount Misry, Genl. Gates moved his Quarters. by express we hear of ye Enemy' coming to Fort Stanwix &c.

13 I moved to Mr. Fields.

14 an 18 Pr split at Tarrytown & killd one man, after firing 5 Shot the Shipping went down the river, had Acct of the French fleet.

15 went to Kings ferry in a Whale boat from tarrytown & Returned in it.

16 from Tarrytown to head Quarters Col. Sears & Col. Willit lodgd with me.

17 went to Tarry Town. 4 ps of Cannon arrived by water at that place.

18 Rode round among the Workmen.

19 Dined with Col. Graton.

20 Genl. Gates returned to camp with sigl wagons went to see Genl. Washington at

21 went to Tarry Town

22 Genl. Nixon & Person[161] went down with there Briggades to Mile squair.

23 the detachment returnd with 170 Cows & a great No. of Horses, hogs &c & women. I rode with Genl. Washington thro King street, took a View of the sound, & round Camp & dind with him.

24 Col Hayzen & a No. of officers dind with me. Genl. Washington' Army moved into the Front of Genl. Gates & took the New position.

25 Genl. De portee[162] & others dind with me.

26 went to hear Dr Smith preach. dind with genl. De portee

27 Set a party of Coaliers to work dind with Genl. Wayne, Col. Stewart[163] & others.

28 Rode round among the workmen.

29 among the workmen at ye Qr. M. Genls.

30 dind at home Genl. De Collee[164] breakfasted with us Lt Dorothy[165] came up.

31 at home & at Qr. M. Genl.

August 1 Rode round among the Workn.

2 at home.

3 & 4 among the workmen.

5 a No. of desarters came in Col. Laradier went down with the detachment.

6 Col. Hazen Capt. Brewer dind with me.

7 Dind with Genl DeCall,[166] Genl. De Portell[167] & seven other French Genln. 2 Officers came in.

8 dind at home, heard of the English burning 3 of there own Frigates at Rhodiland & that place blocked up by the French fleet.

9 16 desarters came in from New York.

10 Recd bad provisions & sent it back.

11 Rode round to all the workmen

12 Mr Dorothy took a letter & 2lb Tea for Mrs B.

13 heard of Genl. Sullivans landing his troops on Rhodisland & of the French Fleet going from the harbour

of Rodiland in parsuit of Lord Hows[168] Fleet. Raind & cold

14 15 & 16   at home very busy giving orders to the workmen. Rainey weather.

17   11 Prisoners brought out for Execution, one Shot the others Reprieved untill Friday, a Vast Concorse of People.

18   went to the purchase in forenoon. Genls Lee,[169] Schuyler, Gates, St Clair, Wayne, Lincoln with there Aids dind with me. Very Sosible.

19   Dind with Colo La Radier[170] in Company with Genls DeKalb,[171] De Portell, La Navil,[172] Cols. 5 & 2 Majrs.

20   White Plains. Dind with Genl St Clair in Compny with Genl. Schuyler, Poor, Morriss, Majr Duor & Morriss.

21   the 10 Prisoners brought out to the place of Execution where they all recd a pardon & ordered to join yr Regts. dind this Day with Genl. Lee in Compny with Genl. Moriss, Colo Brooks[173] Majr Edwards and others at the Purchase.

22   at home. Miss Katy Tenyke went to ye lines.

23   at home all Day, Dr Wheeler Dind with me.

24   Went to ye Purchase, Setled part of my Ration viz. from 1 Jany to ye 1 June. Dind with Dr. Hale, Col. Read, Silley & heard that the French fleet had got

back to Rodiland & had brought in with them one bumb ketch & a other Vessels they had taken from the English & that Genl. Sullivan had driven the Enemy from 3 of there Redoubts.

25   at home.

26   at home & at Cort Martial.

27   went to Tarrytown. Dind with Genl. Washington. Katy Tenike Hurt.

28   at Home & with the workmen.

29   Summoned to Court Martial on the trial of Genl. St. Clair. attended the Court King Street.

30   at Home all Day A large fleet Sailed thro the Sound towards Rhodisland with a fair wind.

31   Rode to the purchase Hospital.

Septr 1   Rode Round to all the workmen, went to Genl. Gates's got the Commissions for the artificers. heard that a party of our men were cut off by the enemy Near Valentines hill. Capt. Goodall killed or taken, also heard of a battle at Rhodisland. Capt. Goodell taken yesterday.

2   Genls. Putnam & Nixon, Cols. Graton, Putnam,[174] Nixon & Docr. Hitchcock & Smith, Majr. Putnam[175] dind with me. a fine pleasant Day.

3   Dind with Genl. Schuyler & a large Comy.

4   heard that Genl. Sullivan had got of the Island with his army after som considerable loss. at home Colo. Hay wt to Fish Kill. setled with Mr Yancy.

5   Dr Wheeler dind with me.
6   Dind with Genl. Nixon in company with Genl. Lincoln, Colo. Newell & others.
7   Attended Genl. Court Martial on the trial of Genl. St Clair.
8   the Enemy Came out in 2 collums as far as Judg Wards. Took about 30 horses yt were in pasture & took 8 Men & returnd back to there lines. at Court Martial.   Dind with Colo. Putnam, went to the Auditors to settle my Ration Acct. Colo. Kosiusko insulted by Mr Carter.
9   a Rainey Day.   Court M. ajurned in ye Morn.
10   proposed going to Albany, went to Head Qr ters. Court M. adjurned A. M.
11   Setled my Ration Acct. to 1 of June. Genl. Poors, Paterson & Learnards Brigades March with Genl. Gates.
12   at Court Martial. sent of some Smiths to west point & to Terry town.
13   the sick sent of to fish Kill by Land & water. the Pionears Marched in 2 parties to mend Roads to Fish Kill & to Fishburg.
14   at Home & among the Workmen.
15   Mathew Carchight Hanged.
16   the Army marched from White plains in 3 Collums.
17   Rode With Colo. Hay, Majr Cammell to view the Landing at Peeks kill.   Lodgd at Mr Burtsills.

18   Rode with His Exelency to West Point. Dind with ye Company & went round to all the works.   Lodgd at Devenport.

19   Rode to Fish Kill Supt with Colo Hay in Compy with his Exelency & Famy.

20   Breakfasted with them. Went to West point, Dind with Colo. Malcom[176] and Lodgd. Genl. Putnam came over.

21   went to Roberson House with Genl. Putnam, Colo. Gansiforth[177] & others. went up in a boat to Fish Kill in Company with 5 Gentn, heard of the Enemy doing mischief at Germn Flats Taking Cattle &c.

22   went from Colo. Brinkerhoffs to the landing with Capt. Lows carpenters, imbarked with them on bord a Sloop for Albany. they to cut timber at Cuymans for Barracks.

23   Lodgd at Mr.

24   Sailed up the North River. Lodgd 8 miles below Cuymans at Solomon Shirts Cosockey.[178]

25   went up to Albany in a Whail boat.

26   at Albany.   Dind with Genl. Starks.

27   Sunday. at Albany. Dind with Majr Sickles, spent the Evning with Colo. Cammell, Genl Stark, Colo. Butler. Visited the Hospital. Drank Tea with Docr Young & Ladies.

28   Dind at ye Kings Arms with Colo Butler, Cammel,

Mr Taylor & a large Company. afternoon set of down the River. Lodgd at Colo. Nicholses.

29 went to the Carpenters at Cuymans, Dind & Lodged at Mr Blikers. began to load the Sloop with Timber.

20 as I was going in a Canoe aboard of a Sloop coming down the River I was nocked over board by the force of the canoe against the Sloop, but fortunately was soon taken up again.

Octobr 1 Loading the Sloop. Dind with Esqr McCarty.

2 finished Loading the Sloop, the wind high.

3 it Raind, the wind high, the cable parted, lost the anchor, the sloop went on shore, at high water got her off. set sail about 4 o'clock down the River. Lodgd on bord, Kinderhook.

4 Sailed down the River, lodgd on bord

5 got to fish Kill Ferry at Sunrise, went to west point & from thence to Fish Kill

6 at Fish Kill, Waited upon his Exelency.

7 went to Fredricksburgh. Dind at Head Quarters. Lodgd with Genl. Nixon.

8 went to Danbury, Breakfasted with Genl. Gates. Returnd to Fredrixbg dind with Genl. St Clair in Compy with Genl. Schuyler, Wayne, Col. Biddle, Col. Palfary,[179] Mrs Biddle & Miss Shaw & others. Lodgd with Colo. Pettit.

9   Rode to Fish Kill to Colo. Brinkerhorp.
10 Dind at Colo Hays. a Rainey Day.
11 at Home all Day. a Great Rain.
12 went to the Office in town.
13 Rode with Genl. St Clair & Dr Treat to New Winsor.[180] Lodgd at Mr Ellises.
14 to West Point. Lodgd Colo. Kosiusko.
15 Rode to Genl. Putnams & then to Fish Kill to my old lodgings. Sent Lieut Bacon to Albany on business.
16 at Home. Drank Tea with Colo. Smith.
17 dind with Colo. Hay & Large Company.
18 at Fish Kill.
19 dind. at Home.
20 Went to Fredrisburgh.
21 Returnd to Colo. Brinkerhoffs. Genl. Green[181] & Colo Putnam lodgd Supt & Breakfasted with me.
22 Rode to Town with Genl. Green. Capt Robison of Boxford has Oliver Hows Wages for 1776.
23 Rode to Manderals. Dind with Genl. Putnam. Majr Putnam returnd from N. York. there is no prospect of the Enemy leaving that place this winter. I Returnd to F Kill.
24 Moved over to Fredricksburg. Lodgd at David Akins.
25 Moved to Mr Shermans for Qrters
26 Dind with Colo Samll Hay.[182]

27 Colo Stevens & Dr Cook Dind with me.
28 Capt. Wm Prichard dind with me swapt H.
29 at Home Capt. Bruen[183] dind with me
30 Dind with His Exelency.
31 went to Qr M. Genl Store got cloths for the workmen. it Raind.

Novr 1 at the park. Drank Tea with Mrs Stevens on Quaker Hill at Dr Morgans.
2 at Home went to the Park.
3 got a Warrant for Retained Ration. Colo Ward, Col. Scammel, Colo Stevens, Majr Gilman, Capt Winslow dind with me. Lt. Welsh Lodgd.
4 paid of the Colliers Taylor M cloths.
5 Lt Welsh dind with me & Bugby.
6 Capt. Low came from Cuymans with Lt Bacon & returnd to Fish kill. Capt. Bruen Dind with me.
7 Colo Grey,[184] Majr Shaw & Kane dind with me Genl. Putnam, Colo Bland, Majr Gimason Lodgd with me.
8 Went to meeting at the park.
9 at Home. 2 Virgina Copls Lodgd with me.
10 Hunting squirrils. Dind with Majr. Kean.
11 a Very Rainey Day, at home all Day.
12 Genl Wayne, Col Steward, Colo S Hay, Majr. Dind with me.
13 Dind with Genl. Wayne in Company with Genl

Washington & family & a No of other officers. heard of a 64 G Sh Cast away.

14 Dind at Judg Wards with a No Artillery officers. Capt Mills & Low at my house.

15 at Home Colo Hay Lodgd with me.

16 Capts Eaton & Thayer Dind with me. they took there orders to raise Company.

17 Lt Hall & Blanchard Dind with me.

18 Capt. Pendelton[185] Dind with me.

19 at Home, it snowed.

20 had orders to move. Dind with Capt. Post. Lt. Bacon went to Danby.

21 at Home went to the Paymasters.

22 Movd the Wagon to peeks Kill, went myself to Fish Kill Lodgd Supt & Break with Col Hay. went to west point.

23 Lodgd with Colo Kosiusko. Genl. Nixons Brigade at Continl Villege.

24 Went to picks Kill Lodgd Mr Burtsells, Dind with Colo Malcom, West Point.

25 Rode to Continental Villedge, Lt Parkes Company went to work there.

26 Rode to Cont Village Mrs. Knox, Majr Shaw dind with me. Rode to Kings Ferry.

27 Rode to Colo Nixons at the Villeage.

28 the Virginia Troops Crossing the ferry.

29 Went down to the ferry, Pensylvania Crossing.

30 the Artillery Crossed.

Decr 1 The Qr M G & His Exelency Bage Crossed.

I was at the ferry all Day.
2 was at the ferry all Day. } without Victuals or Drink.

3 went to see Genl. Mc Dougal[186] Colo Gorivon.[187] at home afternoon.

4 Went to west point with Gen McDougal, Dind with Colo Kosiusko, Genl Paterson & others. heard the shiping was coming up the River, went to Kings Ferry, there all night. the Stores removed.

5 the Enemy landed at W. Side ye ferry & then went down the River without doing much mischief.

6 Colo Hay with the Pensyla troops crossed the River for head Quarters.

7 at Genl. McDougals, our flag Returnd.

8 Colo Greaton & the Brigade Returnd.

9 went to Genl. McDougals.

10 a very Rainey Day, at Home all Day.

11 Set out for head Quarters, rode to the Ferry, the wind high, no crossing till Just night, went over, fed our horses at Majr Cass stopt at Colo hawk Hays. Rode to Judg Coles Lodgd.

12 Rode to pumpton, Dind at Capt. Schuyler, Rode to Mr Jacoburds.

13 It Raind hard in the morning & foggy all Day ley by till monday had a fine Day.

14 Rode to camp 40 miles Rariton Lodgd at Mr. Tenyk.

15 breakfasted with his Exelency. Dind with Colo Scammell.

16 Rode thro & round the incampment Dind with His Exelency. moved to Mr. Michael Hogoman.

17 went to genl. Greens & Genl. Waynes.

18 Genl. Waynes 2 Brigades moved over to the south side the Rariton.

19 went to Capt Pendeltons Camp & to the other Artificers. Capt. Mills came in.

20 with Capt. Low setled with Capt. Eaton & Qr M Blanchard Dind at

21 at Bown Brook.[188]

22 at Capt Pendeltons & Bruens.

23 Visited all the Artificers.

24 at Genl Greens & at Bown Brook.

25 Dind with the Artificer Officers.

26 Very Cold Day Recd orders to impress Shops & Coal for the Smiths.

27 Dind with My Lord Sterling.

28 Dind with Capt Pendelton.

29 Dind with Majr Claibourne[189] at Genl Greens with Colo Tompson & Bidell.

30 Fast Day pleasant men at work

31 went to pluckumin[190] Dind wh Capt. N.

Jany 1 1779 Dind with the Artificers Officers at Capt Pendeltons.

2 Dind at Home with Docr Griffis, Majr Storer & Docr.

3 Sunday the smiths out of coal, it raind. at home afternoon.

4 Went round to the workmen. Dind with My Lord Sterling.

5 My Horse Died. it Snowd

6 Dind at home heard ye Cork fleet being taken by Admiral De Estang.[191]

7 Capt Millses House Burnt & he fortun escaped, it took fire in ye night

8 Rode to Bown Brook & to Capt Parker Camp went to ye Qr M. Y. Stores

9 All my men in Hutts. delivered in ye Tent.

10 Sunday at home all Day. Lieut Jewet Discharged.

11 Dind at Home, Supt with Colo Thompson

12 All the officers of ye Artificers supt to geather at Lieut Littles. house warming

13 the Artificers Mustered went to

14 15 16 in camp with the workmen

17 went to meeting to hear Rd Mr Hole

NOTES

NOTES

THE following notes refer to some of the persons and places, the names of which occur in the foregoing Journal. It would have been easy to have made the references more numerous than they are and the notes more extended. The design has not been, however, to swell the list beyond its real purpose, which is to give a brief record of some of the leading persons named, mainly officers in the Continental service; and to locate some of the places which, at the time, were known by names different from those which they now bear. This has not been done with reference to all the names of persons and places mentioned; nor has the Editor deemed it necessary to add notes in the case of well known leading characters in Revolutionary history. In several instances, also, the Editor has not been able to give records of persons mentioned or to locate places. The student of history can, however, in most cases, add to the records given a full account of the person named by consulting a good Biographical Dictionary, while for the names of places, now obsolete, local histories will complete the information.

DECEMBER, 1775.

[1] Oliver: Oliver Howe, Col. Baldwin's body servant.

[2] Cobble Hill: This is where recently was the McLean Asylum for the Insane in Somerville.

[3] Col. Glover: John Glover, Colonel of Massachusetts Regiment 19 May to December, 1775; Colonel of 14th Continental Infantry 1st January, 1776; Brigadier General Continental Army 21st February, 1777.

[4] Lechmor Point: Now East Cambridge; so called because owned by the Lechmor family.

[5] Genl. Putnam: Israel Putnam, born at Danvers, Mass., in 1718; served in the French and Indian war; Lieut. Colonel in Lexington alarm April, 1775; in 1775 was given command of the Connecticut forces; was at the battle of Bunker Hill; held the command at New York, and in 1777 was appointed to the defence of the Highlands on the Hudson; Colonel 3rd Connecticut 1st May, 1775; Major General Continental Army 19th June, 1775. He died in 1790.

[6] Major Durkee: John Durkee, Major 3rd Connecticut 1st May, 1775 Lieut. Colonel 20th Continental Infantry 1st January, 1776.

JANUARY, 1776.

[7] Major Knowlton: Thomas Knowlton, Major 20th Continental Infantry 1st January, 1776.

[8] Prospect Hill: In Somerville, north from Cobble Hill.

[9] Lieut. Gray: Ebenezer Gray, 2nd Lieutenant 3rd Connecticut 1st May to 19th December, 1775; 1st Lieutenant and Quartermaster 20th Continental Infantry 1st January, 1776; Brigade Major to General Par-

sons' Brigade 31st August to December, 1776; Major 6th Connecticut 1st January, 1777; Lieut. Colonel 15th October, 1778.

[10] Major Richard Cary: Brigade Major 15th August, 1775; Lieut. Colonel and Aide-de-Camp to Gen. Washington 21st June, 1776.

[11] Captain Abbot: Joshua Abbot, Captain 1st New Hampshire Regiment 24th April to December, 1775; Captain 5th Continental Infantry 1st January to 31st December, 1776.

[12] Col. Little: Colonel Massachusetts Regiment 19th May to December, 1775; Colonel 12th Continental Infantry 1st January to 31st December, 1776.

[13] Col. Serjant: Paul Dudley Sargent, Colonel of Massachusetts Regiment May to December, 1775; Colonel of 16th Continental Infantry 1st January to 31st December, 1776.

[14] Father Parkman: Rev. Ebenezer Parkman, of Westboro, Mass.

[15] Col. Gridley: Colonel Massachusetts Artillery Regiment 2d May, 1775; wounded at Bunker Hill; Colonel and Chief Continental Artillery 29th September to 17th November, 1775; Colonel and Chief Engineer June, 1775, to August, 1776; in service to 1st January, 1781, then retired.

[16] Genl. Heath: William Heath, Major General Massachusetts Militia 20th June 1775; Brigadier General Continental Army 22d June, 1775; Major General 9th August, 1776.

[17] Gen. Gates: Horatio Gates was born in Essex, England; served under General Braddock and on the peace of 1763, retired to an estate in Virginia. In 1775 was Adjutant General and in 1776 Commander of the army which had just retired from Canada; compelled the surrender of Burgoyne at Saratoga, October, 1777; died April 10, 1806.

FEBRUARY, 1776.

[18] Wistown: Probably what is now called Weston.

[19] Shrewsbury: A town north of Worcester.

[20] Capt. Upham: Phineas Upham of Brookfield, who was very active in revolutionary affairs.

[21] Col. Buckminster: William Buckminster, Lieut. Colonel of Brewer's Massachusetts Regiment May, 1775; Lieut. Colonel 6th Continental Infantry 1st January, 1776.

[22] Dorchester Point: What is now called City Point in South Boston.

[23] The Castle: Castle Island, Boston Harbor.

[24] Col. Learnard: Ebenezer Learned, Colonel of a Massachusetts Regiment 19th May to December, 1775; Colonel 3rd Continental Infantry 1st January, 1776; Brigadier General Continental Army 2d April, 1777.

MARCH, 1776.

[25] Dorchester Hills: What is now South Boston.

[26] Gen. Thomas: John Thomas, Colonel of Massachusetts Regiment May, 1775; Brigadier General Continental Army 22d June, 1775; Major General 6th March, 1776.

[27] Nook Hill: An eminence at the extremity of Dorchester Neck, separated from Boston by a narrow arm of the harbor; Dorchester Heights commanded Nook Hill and the town itself.

[28] Genl. Ward: Artemas Ward, Colonel of Massachusetts Regiment 23rd May, 1775; Major General Continental Army 17th June, 1775; resigned April 23rd, 1776; on duty till 20th September, 1776.

[29] Rev. Saml. Baldwin: Cousin to Colonel Jeduthan Baldwin.

[30] John Adams: Second President of the United States; led the protest against the Stamp Act; was a delegate from Massachusetts to the first Continental Congress; proposed the election of Washington as Commander-in-chief of the Continental Army and was "the colossus of the debate" on the Declaration of Independence. Died July 4, 1826.

[31] Lt. Scott: William Scott, 2d Lieut. of Sargent's Massachusetts

Regiment May, 1775; 1st Lieut. 16th Continental Infantry 1st January to 31st December, 1776.

³² Fairfield: On Long Island Sound, southwest of Bridgeport, Conn.

³³ Lord Stirling: William Alexander, was born in New York in 1726. Being considered by many rightfully entitled to an earldom in Scotland, which he vainly endeavored to obtain, he was by courtesy called Lord Stirling. He opened the battle of Long Island where he commanded a brigade. He was with Washington at the battle of Brandywine in 1777, fighting side by side with Sullivan and Lafayette, and led one of the divisions of Washington's army at the battle of Monmouth. He died in 1783.

³⁴ Col. Groton: John Greaton, Colonel of Heath's Massachusetts Regiment 19th May, 1775; Colonel 1st July, 1775; Colonel 24th Continental Infantry 1st January, 1776; Colonel 3rd Massachusetts 1st November, 1776.

April, 1776.

³⁵ Gov. Trion: Royal Governor of New York.

³⁶ Col. Mifflin: Thomas Mifflin, Major and Aide-de-Camp to General Washington 4th July, 1775; Major and Quartermaster General Continental Army 14th August, 1775, with rank of Colonel 22d of December, 1775; with rank of Brigadier General 16th May, 1776.

³⁷ Genl. Sullivan: John Sullivan, Brigadier General Continental Army 22d June, 1775; Major General 9th August, 1776; taken prisoner 27th August, 1776; exchanged December, 1776. Resolution of Congress voted him thanks, passed September, 1778, for victory of August 29th, 1778.

³⁸ Col. Prescott: William Prescott, Colonel of a Massachusetts Regiment May to December, 1775; Colonel 7th Continental Infantry 1st January to 31st December, 1776.

³⁹ Fort Montgomery: West side of Hudson river, just above Peekskill.

[40] Capt. Badlam: Stephen Bodlam, Captain of Knox Regiment Continental Artillery 10th December, 1775, to December, 1776.

[41] New Winsor: West bank of Hudson, just below Newburg.

[42] Newboro: Probably now Newburg.

[43] Powcapsey: Poughkeepsie.

[44] Livingstone Manor: Livingston Manor was a tract of land granted by government to Robert Livingston, who came to America from Scotland in 1675. It embraced a large portion of what are now the counties of Dutchess and Columbia, in the state of New York. The original grant was confirmed by a royal charter of George I, in 1715, creating the Manor and Lordship of Livingston.

[45] Col. Paterson: John Paterson, Colonel of Massachusetts Regiment April to December, 1775; Colonel 15th Continental Infantry 1st January, 1776; Brigadier General Continental Army 21st February, 1777, to close of war; Brevet Major General 30 September, 1783.

[46] Col. Bond: William Bond, Lieut. Colonel Gardner's Massachusetts Regiment 2d June, 1775; Colonel 3rd July to December, 1775; Colonel 25th Continental Infantry 1st January, 1776.

[47] Col. Poor: Thomas Poor, Major of Frye's Massachusetts Regiment 20th May to December, 1775; Lieut. Colonel 5th Continental Infantry 1st January to 31st December, 1776.

[48] Col. Livingstone: James Livingstone, Colonel 1st Canadian Regiment 20th November, 1776.

[49] Cohoes: At the junction of the Hudson and Mohawk Rivers.

[50] Dr. Mchensey: Samuel Mackenzie, Surgeon of 2d Pennsylvania Battalion 30th March, 1776; taken prisoner at Three Rivers 8th June, 1776.

MAY, 1776.

[51] Fort Miller: On Hudson river, south from Fort Edward.

[52] Fort Edward: On Hudson river, south from Lake George.

NOTES 151

⁵³ Genl. Schuyler: Major General Continental Army 19th January, 1775; resigned 19th April, 1779.

⁵⁴ Sabbath Day Point: On west shore of Lake George.

⁵⁵ Col. St. Clair: Arthur St. Clair, Colonel Pennsylvania Militia 1775; Colonel 2d Pennsylvania Battalion 3rd January, 1776; Brigadier General Continental Army 9th August, 1776; Major General 19th February, 1777.

⁵⁶ St. Johns: On Richelieu river.

⁵⁷ Shambelee: On Richelieu river.

⁵⁸ Sorell: At the junction of the Richelieu and St. Lawrence rivers.

⁵⁹ Col. Antell: Edward Antil, Lieut. Colonel 2d Canadian Regiment 22d January, 1776; taken prisoner.

⁶⁰ Genl. Arnold: Benedict Arnold, Captain in Lexington Alarm April, 1775; appointed by Genl. Washington Colonel Continental Army 1st September, 1775; Colonel 20th Continental Infantry 1st January, 1776, to rank from September 1st, 1775; Brigadier General 10th January, 1776; and Major General 17th February, 1777.

⁶¹ M de la Marquisca: An Assistant Engineer from France.

⁶² Col. Alden: Ichabod Alden, Lieut. Colonel of Cotton's Massachusetts Regiment May to December, 1775; Lieut. Colonel 25th Continental Infantry 1st January, 1776; Colonel 7th Massachusetts November 1st, 1776.

⁶³ Maj. Loring: Jotham Loring, Major of Heath's Massachusetts Regiment May to December, 1775; Major 24th Continental Infantry 1st January to 31st December, 1776; Lieut. Colonel 3rd Massachusetts 1st January, 1777.

⁶⁴ De Shambo: Deschambault, on St. Lawrence river, near Quebec.

⁶⁵ Capt. Bliss: Theodore Bliss, Captain of Patterson's Massachusetts Regiment May to December, 1775; Captain of 15th Continental Infantry 1st January, 1776; taken prisoner near The Cedars 18th May, 1776; released 19th May; again taken prisoner at The Cedars 20th May, 1776.

[66] Major Sherburn: Major 15th Continental Infantry 1st January to 31st December, 1776: taken prisoner near Cedars 20th May, 1776.

[67] The Seeders: The Cedars—on the St. Lawrence river just above Montreal.

[68] Capt. Fish: Nicholas Fish, Lieutenant and Captain, Malcolm's New York Regiment, 1775 and 1776; Major 2d New York 21st November, 1776, served till 3rd June, 1783.

[69] Col. Maxwell: William Maxwell, Colonel 2d New Jersey 8th November, 1775; Brigadier General Continental Army 23rd October, 1776.

JUNE, 1776.

[70] Three Rivers: On St. Lawrence river at mouth of St. Maurice river.

[71] Col. Dehaws: John Philip De Haas, Major of Pennsylvania Provincials, 1775; Colonel 1st Pennsylvania Battalion 22d January, 1776; Colonel 2d Pennsylvania 25th October, 1776, to rank from January 22d, 1776.

[72] Capt. Butler: Joseph Butler, Captain of Nixon's Massachusetts Regiment May to December, 1775; Captain 4th Continental Infantry 1st January to 31st December, 1776.

[73] St. Ours: a small place on the Richelieu River.

[74] Col. Irving: William Irving, Colonel 6th Pennsylvania Battalion 9th January, 1776; taken prisoner at Three Rivers 8th June, 1776; paroled 3rd August, 1776; exchanged May 6th, 1778.

[75] Genl. Burgoyne: John Burgoyne, Commander-in-chief of the English forces in America.

[76] Col. Vorce: Joseph Vose, Lieutenant Colonel of the 24th Continental Infantry 1st January to 31st December, 1776; Colonel 1st Massachusetts 1st January, 1777.

[77] Col. Hazen: Moses Hazen was Lieutenant in British army on half pay when appointed Colonel 2d Canada Regiment 22d January, 1776.

NOTES 153

⁷⁸ St. Trace: On Richelieu River.
⁷⁹ Oile of Noix: Isle aux Noix.
⁸⁰ Iron Point: Point O'Fray.

JULY, 1776.

⁸¹ Chimney Point: In Vermont, on east shore of Lake Champlain.

⁸² Skeensboro: Now Whitehall, at the head of Lake Champlain.

⁸³ Col. Wayne: Anthony Wayne, Colonel 4th Pennsylvania Battalion 3rd January, 1776; Brigadier General Continental Army 21st February, 1777.

⁸⁴ Genl. Waterbury: David Waterbury, Colonel 5th Connecticut 1st May to 13 December, 1775; Brigadier General Connecticut State troops 3rd June, 1776; taken prisoner at Valcours Island 11 October, 1776, exchanged October, 1780.

⁸⁵ Col. Johnston: Francis Johnston, Lieutenant Colonel 4th Pennsylvania Battalion 4th January, 1776; Colonel 5th Pennsylvania 27th September, 1776; retired 17th January, 1781.

⁸⁶ Col. Ogden: Matthias Ogden, served as a volunteer in the expedition to Canada and was wounded at Quebec, 31st December, 1775; Lieutenant Colonel 1st New Jersey 7th March, 1776; Colonel 1st January, 1777.

⁸⁷ Mount Independence: In Vermont, on shore of Lake Champlain, just East of Ticonderoga.

AUGUST, 1776.

⁸⁸ Capt. Bigelow: John Bigelow, served as a volunteer under Arnold at Ticonderoga in May, 1775; Captain Independant Company Connecticut Infantry 19th January to December, 1776.

⁸⁹ Capt. Wilson: James Armstrong Wilson, Captain 6th Pennsylvania Battalion 9th January, 1776; taken prisoner 24th July, 1776 on Sorell River, Canada, exchanged 1777.

[90] Major Stewart: Walter Stewart, Captain 3rd Pennsylvania Battalion 5th January, 1776; Major and Aide-de-Camp to Genl. Gates 7th June, 1776.

[91] Col. Courtland: Philip Van Courtland, Lieut. Colonel 4th New York 30th June, 1775; Colonel 2d New York 21st November, 1776, to end of war.

[92] Col. Hartly: Thomas Hartley, Lieut. Colonel 6th Pennsylvania Battalion 10th January, 1776; Colonel of one of the sixteen additional Continental Regiments 1st January, 1777.

[93] Capt. Bush: Lewis Bush, 1st Lieutenant 6th Pennsylvania Battalion 9th January, 1776; Captain 24th January, 1776; transferred to Hartley's additional Continental Regiment 13th January, 1777.

[94] Lieut. Whitcomb: There were two Lieutenant Whitcombs in Bedel's Regiment of New Hampshire Rangers — Benjamin and Elisha.

[95] Genl. Carlton: In command of the British forces in Canada.

[96] Genl. Brickett: James Brickett, Lieut. Colonel of Frye's Massachusetts Regiment 20th May, 1775; wounded at Bunker Hill; served subsequently as Brigadier General of Massachusetts Militia.

[97] Col. Phinney: Edmund Phinney, Colonel of a Massachusetts Regiment July to December, 1775; Colonel 18th Continental Infantry 1st January to 31st December, 1776.

SEPTEMBER, 1776.

[98] Capt. Crague: Charles Craig, 1st Lieutenant of Thompson's Pennsylvania Rifle Regiment, 25th June, 1775; Captain 9th November, 1775; Captain 1st Continental Infantry 1st January to 31st December, 1776.

[99] Rev. Mr. Hitchcock: Chaplain 3rd Continental Infantry 13th March to 31st December, 1776; Chaplain 10th Massachusetts 1st January, 1777.

[100] Col. Lewis: Morgan Lewis, Colonel and Deputy Quartermaster General Northern Department 12th September, 1776, to close of war.

[101] Otter Creek: A stream rising in Southern Vermont and flowing north into Lake Champlain.

OCTOBER, 1776.

[102] Lt. Dallas: Archibald Dallas 2d Lieutenant 1st New Jersey 9th December, 1775.

[103] Major Butler: William Butler, Captain 2d Pennsylvania Battalion 5th January, 1776; Major 7th September, 1776; Lieut. Colonel 4th Pennsylvania 30th September, 1776.

[104] Capt. Fassit: John Fassit, 1st Lieutenant Green Mountain Boys 27th July, 1775; 1st Lieutenant Warner's Additional Continental Regiment 5th July, 1776; Captain 16th September, 1776; cashiered 16th October, 1776.

[105] Onion River: A river rising near Montpelier and flowing west into Lake Champlain.

[106] Capt. Rew: John Rew, Regimental Quartermaster 6th Pennsylvania 7th December, 1777.

[107] Dr. Canada: Samuel Kennedy, Surgeon 4th Pennsylvania Battalion 24th February to 31st December, 1776.

[108] Dr. Johnson: Robert Johnson, Surgeon to 6th Pennsylvania Battalion 9th January, 1776, to January, 1777.

NOVEMBER, 1776.

[109] Col. Dayton: Elias Dayton, Colonel 3rd New Jersey 18th January, 1776; transferred to 2d New Jersey 1st January, 1781; Brigadier General Continental Army 7th January, 1783.

[110] Col. Wood: Joseph Wood, Captain 2d Pennsylvania Battalion November, 1775; Major 4th January, 1776; Lieut. Colonel 29th July,

1776; Colonel 7th September, 1776; wounded at Lake Champlain 11th October, 1776; Colonel 3rd Pennsylvania Regiment January, 1777, to rank from 30th September, 1776.

[111] Capt. Romanes: Bernard Romanes, Captain Independent Pennsylvania Artillery Company 8th February, 1776.

[By a typographical error, there is no reference to Capt. Church, third line from the top, page 88. This should be [112]. Capt. Church was Captain of the 4th Pennsylvania Battalion 5th January, 1776; Major September, 1777, to rank from March, 1777.]

[113] Major Stevens: 1st Lieutenant Company of Rhode Island Artillery May, 1775; Captain of Knox's Regiment Continental Artillery 10th December, 1775; Major Independent Battalion of Artillery 9th November, 1776; Brevet Major Continental Army 27th May, 1777; his battalion annexed to 3rd Continental Artillery fall of 1778; Brevet Lieut. Colonel Continental Army 30th April, 1778, "in consideration of his services as commanding officer of Artillery in the Northern Department during two campaigns."

[114] Majr. Fraser: Persifer Fraser, Captain 11th Pennsylvania Battalion 5th January, 1776; Major 3rd October, 1777, to rank from 24th September, 1776.

[115] Capt. Cristy: John Christie, 1st Lieutenant 4th Pennsylvania Battalion 5th January, 1776; Captain 5th Pennsylvania 23rd October, 1776.

[116] Stillwater: On the Hudson river.

[117] Lt. Col. Fisher: John Fisher, Captain 2nd New York 28th June, 1775; Major 3rd New York 8th March, 1776; Lieut. Colonel Nicholson's New York Regiment 21st June to November, 1776.

JANUARY, 1777.

[118] Maj. Brown: Jacob Brown, Major 18th Continental Infantry 1st January to 31st December, 1776.

NOTES 157

[119] Squam: On Cape Ann, Massachusetts.

[120] Capt. Low: Jacob Low, Ensign of 8th Continental Infantry 1st January to 31st December, 1776; Captain of Baldwin's Artificer Regiment 16th December, 1776.

[121] Capt. McNeal: Joseph McNiel, Captain of Wigglesworth's Regiment Massachusetts Militia in 1776.

FEBRUARY, 1777.

[122] Blanford: In southern part of western Massachusetts.

[123] Tithingham: Probably Tyringham, Massachusetts.

[124] Great Barrington: In southwestern Massachusetts.

[125] Canderhook: Kinderhook, east side Hudson river, just above Hudson.

[126] Capt. Alexander: Nathaniel Alexander, 2nd Lieutenant of Brewer's Massachusetts Regiment May to December, 1775; 1st Lieutenant 6th Continental Infantry 1st January, 1776; Captain 13th Massachusetts 13th November, 1776.

MARCH, 1777.

[127] Dr. McCray: Stephen McCrea, Surgeon 2nd New York 28th June, 1775, to January, 1776; Hospital Surgeon October, 1776.

APRIL, 1777.

[128] Maj. Rian: Michael Ryan, 2d Lieutenant 4th Pennsylvania Battalion 5th January, 1776; Regimental Adjutant 15th March, 1776; Brigade Major St. Clair's Brigade 17th September, 1776; to General Wayne 21st May, 1777, to 13th June, 1779.

[129] Col. Long: Peirce Long, Colonel New Hampshire Militia 1776 to 1778.

[130] Col. Mooney: Hercules Mooney, Lieut. Colonel and Colonel New Hampshire Militia 1776 and 1777.

158   NOTES

[131] Capt. Nichols: Francis Nichols, 2d Lieutenant of Thompson's Pennsylvania Rifle Battalion 25th June, 1775; taken prisoner at Quebec 31st December, 1775, exchanged 10th October, 1776; Captain 9th Pennsylvania 16th December, 1776, to rank from January 1, 1776.

[132] Col. Basset: Barakiah Bassett, Lieut. Colonel 14th Massachusetts 19th November, 1776.

[133] Willsboro: On the west shore of Lake Champlain.

[134] Col. Marshall: Thomas Marshall, Major 3rd Virginia 13th February, 1776; Lieut. Colonel 13th August, 1776; Colonel 21st February, 1777; resigned December 4th, 1777.

[135] Col. Francis: Ebenezer Francis, Captain of Mansfield's Massachusetts Regiment May to December, 1775; Colonel 11th Massachusetts Regiment 6th November, 1776.

[136] Capt. Levensworth: Eli Levensworth, Captain 7th Connecticut 6th July to 10th December, 1775; Captain 19th Continental Infantry 1st January to 31st December, 1776; Captain 6th Connecticut 1st January, 1777.

MAY, 1777.

[137] Col. Van Dyck: Captain 2d New York 28th June, 1775; Lieut. Colonel 1st New York 21st November, 1776.

[138] Rogers Rock: On west side Lake George at the north end of Lake.

[139] Col. Kosiosko: Tadeusz Kosciusko (Kosiosko), a Polish patriot, born in Lithuania in 1746; came to this country with the French fleet in 1777, and fought for the colonies, becoming a Major General. He died October 15, 1817.

[140] Col. Wilkison: James Wilkison, served as volunteer in Thompson's Pennsylvania Rifle Battalion 9th September, 1775, to March, 1776; Captain 2d Continental Infantry March, 1776, to rank from 9th September, 1775; served on staff of General Greene November, 1775,

NOTES 159

to April, 1776; Aide-de-Camp to Genl. Arnold 2d June to 17th July, 1776; Brigade Major 20th July, 1776, and on the staff of General Gates from December 13th, 1776; Lieut. Colonel Hartley's Additional Continental Regiment 12th January, 1777.

[141] Maj. Hull: William Hull, Captain 3rd Massachusetts 6th July to December, 1775; Captain 19th Continental Infantry 1st January to 31st December, 1776; Major 8th Massachusetts 1st January, 1777.

[142] Capt. Wilcott: Jarius Wilcox, was 1st Lieutenant Baldwin's Regiment 1st January, 1777.

[143] Lt. Liford: Thomas Liford, 2d Lieutenant 2d New Hampshire 27th May to December, 1775; 1st Lieutenant 8th Continental Infantry 1st January, 1776; 1st Lieutenant Whitcomb's New Hampshire Rangers 4th November, 1776, to December, 1779.

JUNE, 1777.

[144] Maj. Armstrong: John Armstrong, served as volunteer in the Canada expedition to Quebec, 1775; Major and Aide-de-Camp to General Mercer to 3rd January, 1777.

JULY, 1777.

[145] Col. Bellows: Benjamin Bellows, Colonel New Hampshire Militia in 1777 and 1778.

[146] Castleton: In western part of Vermont.

[147] Genl. Nixon: John Nixon, Captain of Company Minute Men at Lexington; Colonel of Massachusetts Regiment 19 May to December, 1775; Colonel 4th Continental Infantry 1st January, 1776; Brigadier General Continental Army 9th August, 1776.

[148] Lieut. Hitchings: William Hutchings, Ensign 4th Continental Infantry 1st January to 31st December, 1776; 2nd Lieutenant 1st New Hampshire 8th November, 1776; 1st Lieutenant 5th March, 1778; resigned 2nd June, 1779.

[149] Genl. Fellows: John Fellows, Colonel Massachusetts Regiment May to December, 1775; Brigadier General Massachusetts Militia 1776 to 1780.

August, 1777.

[150] Fort Stanwix: Albany, New York.

[151] Col. Wiglesworth: Edward Wigglesworth, Colonel Massachusetts Militia 1776; Colonel 13th Massachusetts 1st January, 1777.

[152] Genl. Lincoln: Benjamin Lincoln, Major General Continental Army 19th February, 1777; wounded at Saratoga 7th October, 1777. Resolutions of thanks passed by Congress to Major General Gates and Major Generals Lincoln and Arnold.

[153] Gov. Clinton: Sir Henry Clinton, born about the year 1738; he came to America in 1775 and fought at Bunker Hill; was knighted for his services under General Howe. After Burgoyne's surrender in 1778, Clinton succeeded Howe as Commander-in-Chief. He resigned his commission and returned to England in 1781 and died at Gibraltar in 1795.

[154] Capt. Goodell: Nathan Goodale, Lieutenant of Brewer's Regiment May to December, 1776; 1st Lieutenant 13th Continental Infantry 1st January to 31st December, 1776; Captain 5th Massachusetts 1st January, 1777; taken prisoner 30th August, 1778, exchanged 9th October, 1780.

September, 1777.

[155] Col. Morgan: Daniel Morgan, Captain of Company of Virginia Riflemen July, 1775; taken prisoner at Quebec 31st December, 1775; Colonel 11th Virginia 12th November, 1776.

October, 1777.

[156] Major Lithgow: William Lithgow, Major 11th Massachusetts 1st January, 1777.

NOTES

[157] Scotack: On the east side of Hudson river, just below Albany.

[158] Quemans: Coeyman's, west side of Hudson river, opposite Scotack.

JULY, 1778.

[159] Marrineck: Mamaroneck, on Long Island Sound.

[160] Northcastle: East part of New York State, east of Sing Sing.

[161] Genl. Persons: Samuel H. Parsons, Colonel in Lexington alarm; Colonel 6th Connecticut 1st May to 10th December, 1775; Colonel 10th Continental Infantry 1st January, 1776; Brigadier General Continental Army 9th August, 1776.

[162] Genl. De Portee: Louis Lebique DuPortail, Colonel Engineers 8th July, 1777; Chief of Engineers 22d July, 1777; Brigadier General of Engineers 17th November, 1777; appointed Commandant Corps of Engineers and Sappers and Miners 11th May, 1779.

[163] Col. Stewart: Walter Stewart, Captain 3rd Pennsylvania Battalion 5th January, 1776; Major and Aide-de-Camp to General Gates 7th June, 1776; by act of 19th November, 1776, raised to rank of Colonel by brevet and presented with sword value $100; Colonel Pennsylvania State Regiment 17th June, 1777; designated 13th Pennsylvania 12th November, 1777; transferred to 2d Pennsylvania 1st July, 1778.

[164] Genl. De Collee:

[165] Lieut. Dorothy: Michael Dougherty, 2d Lieutenant 6th Maryland 10th December, 1776; 1st Lieutenant 12th November, 1776; cashiered 14th April, 1779.

AUGUST, 1778.

[166] Genl. De Call; Probably meant for Gen. De Kalb. (See No. [171].)

[167] Genl. De Portell: See Gen. De Portee above. (No.[162].)

[168] Lord Howe: William Howe was born in 1729; had a command under General Wolfe at Quebec; succeeded General Gage in 1775 as

Commander-in-chief of the British forces in America; commanded at Bunker Hill; took New York; defeated Washington at White Plains and at Brandywine, but was superseded by General Clinton in 1778. In 1799 he succeeded to the viscounty of his brother, Richard, Earl Howe.

[169] Genl. Lee: Charles Lee, Major General Continental Army 17th June, 1775; taken prisoner December 13th, 1776, exchanged May 6th, 1778.

[170] Col. La Radier: Mons. Baileul de la Radiere, Lieut. Colonel Engineers 8th July, 1777; Colonel 17th November, 1777; died 1779.

[171] Genl. De Kalb: John, Baron, born at Huttendorf, Germany, 1721; came to America with LaFayette in 1777, and was appointed a Major General by Congress the same year; served under Washington and was killed at the battle of Camden, August, 1780.

[172] Genl. La Navill: Noirmont de la Neuville, Inspector of the Army under General Gates 14th May, 1778; brevet Brigadier General 14th August, 1778; retired 4th December, 1778, and permitted to return to France.

[173] Col. Brooks: John Brooks, Captain Company Massachusetts Minute Men at Lexington and Concord; Major of Bridge's Massachusetts Regiment May to December, 1775; Major 19th Continental Infantry 1st January, 1776; Lieut. Colonel 8th Massachusetts 1st November, 1776; Lieut. Colonel Commandant 7th Massachusetts 11th November, 1778.

[174] Col. Putnam: Rufus Putnam, Lieut. Colonel of Brewer's Massachusetts Regiment May to December, 1775; Lieut. Colonel 22d Continental Infantry 1st January, 1776; Colonel of Engineers 5th August, 1776; Colonel 5th Massachusetts 1st November, 1776, to rank from 5th August, 1776.

[175] Major Putnam: Israel Putnam, Jr., Captain 3rd Connecticut 1st May, 1775; Major and Aide-de-Camp to General Putnam 22d July, 1775, to 3rd June, 1783.

NOTES 163

[176] Col. Malcolm: William Malcolm, served as Major and Colonel of New York Militia, 1776; Colonel of one of the 16 additional Continental Regiments 30th April, 1777, to 22d April, 1779.

[177] Col. Gansiforth: Peter Gansevoort, Major 2nd New York 30th June, 1775; Lieut. Colonel 19th March, 1776; Colonel 3rd New York 21 November, 1776; Act of 4th October, 1777, thanks of Congress extended him for his defence of Fort Schuyler.

[178] Cosockey: Coxsackie, west side of Hudson river, just above Catskill.

OCTOBER, 1778.

[179] Col. Palfrey: William Palfrey, Major and Aide-de-Camp to General Lee 16th July, 1775; Lieut. Colonel and Aide-de-Camp to General Washington 6th March, 1776; Paymaster General 27th April, 1777, with rank of Lieut. Colonel 9th July, 1776.

[180] New Winsor: West side Hudson river, just south of Newburg.

[181] Genl. Geeen: Nathaniel Greene, Brigadier General Continental Army 22d June, 1775; Major General 9th August, 1776; Quarter Master General 2d March, 1778 to 30th September, 1780.

[182] Col. Sam'l Hay: Captain 6th Pennsylvania Battalion 9th January, 1776; Major 7th Pennsylvania 5th October, 1776; Lieut. Colonel 10th Pennsylvania 21st February, 1778.

[183] Capt. Bruen: Jeremiah Bruen, Captain of Baldwin's Artillery Artificer Regiment.

NOVEMBER, 1778.

[184] Col. Grey: Ebenezer Grey, 2d Lieutenant 3rd Connecticut 1st May to 19th December, 1775; 1st Lieutenant and Regimental Quartermaster 20th Continental Infantry 1st January, 1776; Brigade Major to General Parsons' Brigade 31st August to December, 1776; Major 6th Connecticut 1st January, 1777; Lieut. Colonel 15th October, 1778.

[185] Capt. Pendleton: Captain of Baldwin's Artificer Regiment.

DECEMBER, 1778.

[186] Genl. McDougall: Alexander McDougall, Colonel 1st New York 30th June to November, 1775; Brigadier General Continental Army 9th August, 1776; Major General 20th October, 1777.

[187] Col. Gorivon: Jean Baptiste Obrey de Gouvion, Major of Engineers on staff of General Lafayette 8th July, 1777; Lieut. Colonel 17th November, 1777; brevet Colonel 16th November, 1781; 10th October, 1783, retired.

[188] Bown Brook: Bound Brook, New Jersey.

[189] Capt. Claibourne: Buller Claibourne, 2d Lieutenant 2d Virginia 24th October, 1775; Captain 8th March, 1776, to 27th July, 1777; served subsequently as Brigade Major and Aide-de-Camp to General Lincoln 1779 and 1780.

[190] Pluckumin: Pluckemin, New Jersey.

JANUARY, 1779.

[191] Admiral De Estang: Admiral in command of the English fleet.

RENEWALS 691-4574

DATE DUE

DEC 16			
OCT 0 8			

Demco, Inc. 38-293